THE AIRLINE BUILDERS

TIME
LIFE ®
BOOKS

Other Publications:

HEALTHY HOME COOKING
UNDERSTANDING COMPUTERS
YOUR HOME
THE ENCHANTED WORLD
THE KODAK LIBRARY OF CREATIVE PHOTOGRAPHY
GREAT MEALS IN MINUTES
THE CIVIL WAR
PLANET EARTH
COLLECTOR'S LIBRARY OF THE CIVIL WAR
THE GOOD COOK
WORLD WAR II
HOME REPAIR AND IMPROVEMENT
THE OLD WEST

For information on and a full description of any of the Time-Life
Books series listed above, please write:

Reader Information
Time-Life Books
541 North Fairbanks Court
Chicago, Illinois 60611

*This volume is one of a series that traces the adventure and
science of aviation, from the earliest manned balloon ascension
through the era of jet flight.*

22624

THE AIRLINE BUILDERS

by Oliver E. Allen

AND THE EDITORS OF TIME-LIFE BOOKS

TIME-LIFE BOOKS, ALEXANDRIA, VIRGINIA

Time-Life Books Inc.
is a wholly owned subsidiary of

TIME INCORPORATED

FOUNDER: Henry R. Luce 1898-1967

Editor-in-Chief: Henry Anatole Grunwald
President: J. Richard Munro
Chairman of the Board: Ralph P. Davidson
Corporate Editor: Ray Cave
Group Vice President, Books: Reginald K. Brack Jr.
Vice President, Books: George Artandi

TIME-LIFE BOOKS INC.

EDITOR: George Constable
Executive Editor: George Daniels
Editorial General Manager: Neal Goff
Director of Design: Louis Klein
Director of Editorial Resources: Phyllis K. Wise
Editorial Board: Dale M. Brown, Roberta Conlan,
Ellen Phillips, Donia Ann Steele, Rosalind Stubenberg,
Kit van Tulleken, Henry Woodhead
Director of Research and Photography: John Conrad Weiser

PRESIDENT: Reginald K. Brack Jr.
Executive Vice Presidents: John M. Fahey Jr.,
Christopher T. Linen
Senior Vice President: James L. Mercer
Vice Presidents: Stephen L. Bair, Edward Brash, Ralph J.
Cuomo, Juanita T. James, Wilhelm R. Saake, Robert H.
Smith, Paul R. Stewart, Leopoldo Toralballa

THE EPIC OF FLIGHT

Editorial Staff for *The Airline Builders*
Editor: Jim Hicks
Designer: Donald S. Komai
Chief Researcher: Lois Gilman
Picture Editor: Jane N. Coughran
Text Editors: Russell B. Adams Jr., Richard W. Murphy
Staff Writers: Gus Hedberg, Thomas A. Lewis, Glenn Martin
McNatt, Leslie Marshall
Researchers: Dominick A. Pisano and Diane Bohrer
(principals), Betty Ajemian, Susan Schneider Blair
Assistant Designer: Van W. Carney
Copy Coordinator: Elizabeth Graham
Art Assistant: Anne K. DuVivier
Picture Coordinator: Rebecca C. Christoffersen
Editorial Assistant: Deta D. Follin

Editorial Operations
Copy Chief: Diane Ullius
Editorial Operations: Caroline A. Boubin (manager)
Production: Celia Beattie
Quality Control: James J. Cox (director)
Library: Louise D. Forstall

Correspondents: Elisabeth Kraemer-Singh (Bonn); Dorothy
Bacon, Lesley Coleman (London); Susan Jonas, Lucy T.
Voulgaris (New York); Maria Vincenza Aloisi, Josephine du
Brusle (Paris); Ann Natanson (Rome). Valuable assistance
was also provided by: Janny Hovinga (Amsterdam); Martha
Mader (Bonn); Judy Aspinall, Karin B. Pearce (London);
John Dunn (Melbourne); Carolyn T. Chubet, Miriam Hsia,
Christina Lieberman (New York); M. T. Hirschkoff (Paris);
Mimi Murphy (Rome); Janet Zich (San Francisco);
Jean Bolton (Seattle).

THE AUTHOR
Oliver E. Allen made his first passenger flight
in the open cockpit of an itinerant barnstormer's biplane early in the 1930s, an experience that sparked his interest in aviation. He
is a former series editor and planning director
of Time-Life Books and the author of two
volumes in The Seafarers series, *The Wind-
jammers* and *The Pacific Navigators.*

THE CONSULTANT for The Airline Builders
Richard P. Hallion Jr. is the author of several
books on aviation, including *Legacy of Flight:
The Guggenheim Contribution to American
Aviation.* A member of the faculty of the University of Maryland, Dr. Hallion has also
served as Curator of Science and Technology
at the National Air and Space Museum.

THE CONSULTANTS *for* The Epic of Flight
Melvin B. Zisfein, the principal consultant, is
Deputy Director of the National Air and
Space Museum, Washington. He received
degrees in aeronautical engineering from the
Massachusetts Institute of Technology and
has contributed to many scientific, techno-
logical and historical publications. He is an
Associate Fellow of the American Institute of
Aeronautics and Astronautics.

Charles Harvard Gibbs-Smith, Research Fellow at the Science Museum, London, and
a Keeper-Emeritus of the Victoria and Albert Museum, London, has written or edited
some 20 books and numerous articles on
aeronautical history. In 1978 he served as the
first Lindbergh Professor of Aerospace History at the National Air and Space Museum,
Smithsonian Institution, Washington.

Dr. Hidemasa Kimura, honorary professor at
Nippon University, Tokyo, is the author of
numerous books on the history of aviation
and is a widely known authority on aeronautical engineering and aircraft design. One
plane that he designed established a world
distance record in 1938.

Library of Congress Cataloguing in Publication Data
Allen, Oliver E.
    The airline builders.
    (The Epic of flight)
    Bibliography: p.
    Includes index.
    1. Aeronautics, Commercial — United States — History.
2. Air lines — United States — History. I. Time-Life Books.
II. Title. III. Series: Epic of flight.
HE9803.A3A43   387.7'065'73   80-15249
ISBN 0-8094-3285-4
ISBN 0-8094-3284-6 lib. bdg.
ISBN 0-8094-3283-8 retail ed.

CONTENTS

Enticing travelers into the skies

The sudden explosion of commercial aviation during the years that followed World War I virtually stood mankind's centuries-old experience of long-distance travel on its head. The timesaving possibilities of the service offered by the new industry were staggering, yet so was the task of persuading a skeptical public to use that service.

By 1920, most people in Europe and the United States were familiar with airplanes as noisy machines that performed stunts at air circuses and, during wartime, blasted one another out of the skies. The men who flew the planes were perceived as romantic and daring but short-lived. Changing this widespread impression presented a major challenge to the new air-transport industry. So, holding their stunting and war-making colleagues at arm's length, the early airlines set out to reform the public's image of air travel through a campaign of words and pictures.

"It stands to reason," read a booklet advertising daily noontime flights between London and Paris, "that a means by which you gain a useful morning in London and arrive unjaded in Paris in time to pay an important business call, or with leisure to do a little sight-seeing before dinner, is worthy of some consideration." The force of reason, in this instance, prevailed and the fledgling airline flourished.

Across the Channel, copywriters took a more Gallic tack and appealed to their potential customers' esthetic sense. "Life expands in an aeroplane," read an advertisement for one Paris-London service. "The traveller is a mere slave in a train, and, should he manage to escape from this particular yoke, the car and the ship present him with only limited horizons. Air travel, on the other hand, makes it possible for him to enjoy the 'solitary deserts of infinite space.' The earth speeds below him, with nothing hidden, yet full of surprises. Introduce yourself to your pilot. He is always a man of the world as well as a flying ace."

While such rhapsodic descriptions no doubt attracted some customers, the main thrust of the publicity campaign to introduce a train-riding, steamship-loving public to the advantages of air transport took the form of dramatic, vivid posters like those on the following pages. Through them the airlines projected an image of speed, efficiency and stylish convenience, and the posters became the imaginative windows through which many prospective customers got their first glimpse of the new mode of travel.

Well-wishers wave to a departing Fokker
Trimotor of the Danish national airline, Det
Danske Luftfartselskab, in a 1935 poster.

To stress the speed and punctuality of airline
travel, this late-1920s poster shows an
American consulting his watch at the airport.

Passengers deplane under the looming wing of a Short Scylla in this 1936 poster advertising Imperial Airways.

*Rising from the nose of a stylized airplane,
the Spirit of Flight holds aloft the emblem of
Air France—a winged sea horse.*

A SABENA poster juxtaposes a camel and
a plane to emphasize how the airline linked
Belgium to her African possession.

A SABENA poster juxtaposes a camel and a plane to emphasize how the airline linked Belgium to her African possession.

Occupants of a German coach—and a
greyhound running alongside—all look up
in awe at a passing Lufthansa plane.

DEUTSCHE LUFTHANSA

A glossy United Air Lines DC-3 churns through the skies between the San Francisco and New York world's fairs in 1939.

1

European trailblazers on a cloud-filled frontier

On the morning of January 1, 1914, Mayor A. C. Pheil of St. Petersburg, Florida, settled into the open cockpit of the St. Petersburg-Tampa Airboat Line's 26-foot-long Benoist flying boat. Beside him sat Tony Jannus, the pilot, nattily dressed in white slacks, dark blazer and bow tie. At 10 a.m. Jannus gunned his 75-horsepower engine, skimmed across the placid waters of the St. Petersburg Yacht Basin and took to the air over Tampa Bay; 23 minutes later the plane touched down offshore from Tampa, 18 miles away. The world's first regularly scheduled passenger airline had just completed its inaugural run.

The fledgling carrier was short-lived. It folded with the waning of the Florida tourist season in the spring of 1914 and was not revived. But in its brief span it carried more than 1,200 passengers—at five dollars per flight—without mishap. The line was the vanguard of a long procession of commercial airlines that would arise throughout the world during the post-World War I years. Haltingly at first, and then with growing confidence and speed, these bold new ventures extended their range until they spanned continents and bridged ever-wider ocean barriers. They drastically changed mankind's age-old perceptions of distance and time. Journeys once reckoned in weeks or months came to be calculated in days or even hours, and the whole course of civilization was altered by this swift means of transport for people and goods.

The men who worked these wonders were a mettlesome breed of aviation enthusiasts. Many were wartime pilots so captivated by the freedom of the air that they could not give up flying. Others were aircraft builders intent on devising ever-faster and more efficient planes. Still others were entrepreneurs, aggressive and creative organizers who tenaciously fashioned the great airline enterprises that would one day crisscross nations and girdle the globe.

The first full flowering of commercial aviation did not come in the United States—home though it was of the Wright brothers and of the first scheduled airline—but in England and continental Europe.

At the close of World War I in 1918, the belligerent powers on both sides of the Atlantic Ocean found themselves with an abundance of

Poised to board a five-engined World War I bomber that has been refitted for commercial service, German travelers display an apprehensive curiosity typical of early airline passengers.

aircraft and trained pilots eager to fly them for peacetime purposes. In America, where a fast and efficient railroad system spanned the nation, there was little serious interest in aircraft as a means of transportation. Europe presented a different story. The War had wrecked much of the rail network and at the same time had acquainted Europeans at first hand with the airplane's potential. And there were many heavily traveled routes that railroads could not serve, notably those over water, such as Paris to London. Planes also promised to be convenient for reaching distant colonial outposts and tying the colonies more closely to the motherlands.

Great Britain, France and Germany began their pioneering commercial airline ventures within months of one another, each country making a significant contribution to the development of civil air transport. The Germans—who had operated lighter-than-air Zeppelin routes even before the War—led the way in early 1919 with daily airplane flights between Berlin and Weimar, thus launching Europe's first regularly scheduled passenger carrier and the first in the world to endure. The French inaugurated the first international air service soon afterward when they began making weekly flights between Paris and Brussels. Before the summer was over, the British went the French one better by instituting daily flights on an international route, between London and Paris. With these first steps, the evolution of the major national airlines of Europe was under way.

The driving force behind Great Britain's pioneering aerial enterprise was George Holt-Thomas, a distinguished Edwardian figure with a trim beard set off by a stiff wing collar. A founder of the extremely successful de Havilland Aircraft Company, Holt-Thomas was so confident of a postwar air boom that as early as 1916 he had set up an airline company, calling it Aircraft Transport and Travel, Ltd. As soon as the shooting stopped, he assembled a nondescript collection of de Havilland biplanes and began preparations to put his airline in service. As managing director he appointed another visionary, Sir William Sefton Brancker, who had recently resigned his commission as a major general in the Royal Air Force.

Brancker was a dedicated airman who firmly believed that Britain's postwar future lay in the development of civil aviation. He was also something of an eccentric who delighted in demonstrating that he could eat his monocle (he always carried a spare). Brancker quickly put together a cadre of seasoned men, and on August 25, 1919, an Aircraft Transport pilot and former RAF flier named Bill Lawford took off from the airfield at Hounslow, near London, and headed his single-engined D.H.4a toward the English Channel and Paris.

Lawford's lone passenger on this trailblazing international flight was George Stevenson-Reece, a newspaper reporter who had paid £42 for his round-trip ticket. Decked out in bulky flying togs, Stevenson-Reece took the wave-skimming trip with equanimity and even tried to con-

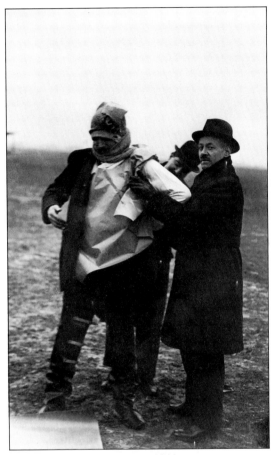

A French airline passenger in 1919 gets a helping hand with his jacket after donning a paper liner to insulate him from the cold. Early airlines provided their travelers with helmets, goggles, gloves and an occasional hot-water bottle for trips in the unheated planes of the day.

.THAYAHT. 22

L'ESSAYAGE A PARIS (CROYDON-BOURGET)
COSTUME POUR TOURISME AÉRIEN, DE MADELEINE VIONNET
TRAVERSÉE À BORD D'UN AVION DE " L'INSTONE AIR LINE "

A 1922 advertisement depicts a woman
in custom-fitted flying togs leaving London
for a two-and-a-half-hour flight to Paris
on an Instone airliner. The outfit was created
by French designer Madeleine Vionnet,
who decided to bring haute couture to air
travel after making her first flight.

vince himself that he enjoyed the sensation of banking as the plane descended to land at the French airfield at Le Bourget after a 2-hour-and-20-minute flight.

Two other Aircraft Transport passengers had somewhat different memories of their flight a few days after Stevenson-Reece's. Gale-force winds and heavy rain lashed England that day, and the London-to-Paris flight was canceled. But chief pilot Jerry Shaw, poised in Paris for the matching flight in the opposite direction, knew nothing of the threatening weather on the other side of the Channel. Shaw took off as scheduled in his D.H.4a transport with the two passengers sitting face to face in the small cabin behind his open cockpit. A tail wind helped him to a rapid passage to Boulogne, on the French coast, but as he droned across the Channel he ran into low clouds and his plane was rocked by turbulent winds.

Shaw made plans to set down at an emergency landing field near the coast and to put his passengers on a train for London. But the winds made such a course impossible, so he flew on toward his home base at Hounslow, slogging through heavy rains and the continuing gale. "Once or twice," he said later, "I gave a passing thought to what was going on in the cabin behind me, for there was no means of communication, and after doing half a turn of a spin over Westerham I wondered if it mattered anyway."

Shaw finally touched down at Hounslow and taxied his craft safely into a hangar. He was amazed to see that his two passengers were smiling broadly as they emerged from the cabin—even though one of them had hit his head on the roof of the plane with such force that all that remained intact of his bowler hat was the rim, which hung loosely around his neck. The other traveler, an Irish priest, gripped a bottle with just enough brandy left in it for a stiff drink for the pilot. "Handing it over," Shaw recalled, the two grateful passengers "thanked me for what they had thought was a wonderful display of stunting."

Holt-Thomas' Aircraft Transport and Travel had no monopoly of the London-to-Paris route. Indeed, on the day that his airline made its first flight to the French capital, another British company, Handley Page Transport Ltd., made a trial run across the Channel to Paris. A month after that, the company expanded and began making regular flights to Brussels three times a week. This second British airline had been founded by Frederick Handley Page, an aircraft manufacturer who had built his country's best-known heavy bombers during the War. Converted to civilian use, the twin-engined planes were fitted out to accommodate as many as 14 passengers in spacious wicker chairs. And the company pioneered in food service to its passengers by offering lunch baskets—for three shillings extra—that contained sandwiches, fruit and chocolate.

Handley Page's stately airliners, based at the company field at Cricklewood, near London, were underpowered and slow, characteristics that helped to establish a British tradition of large, roomy passen-

The short, sad life of a technological dead end

The logic seemed unassailable at the time: If two sets of wings lifted a plane better than one, then every additional set would be just that much better. Thus it was that the Italian firm of Società Aviazione Ing. Caproni went to work in 1919 on its version of the ultimate passenger plane. The result, dubbed the Ca.60, was a flying boat 77 feet long with nine wings, the longest spanning about 100 feet.

In its first trial flight, held on Lake Maggiore on March 3, 1921, the giant craft rose majestically from the water and flew a hundred feet before flopping back down—amid the cheers of Caproni executives. A more rigorous test came the next day, when ballast weighing the equivalent of 60 passengers was loaded aboard. Test pilot Federico Semprini lifted the awkward machine to an altitude of 60 feet, but the load was too much for the eight straining engines. The plane plunged into the lake in a tangle of wires, canvas and splintered wood. Semprini lived to fly again, but Caproni's grand design was permanently shelved.

Bobbing gently on the placid waters of Lake Maggiore, the multiwinged Ca.60 is readied for its ill-fated second test flight.

ger aircraft in which comfort was emphasized over power and speed.

Aircraft Transport and Handley Page were soon joined in their cross-Channel flights by a third organization, The Instone Air Line Ltd. Begun in the fall of 1919 by the steamship concern of S. Instone & Company, the line had at first been used to carry shipping documents and company officials to Paris. Its premier pilot, a celebrated aviator named Frank Barnard, added a jubilant note to his inaugural flight by casting out hundreds of greeting cards as he passed over Boulogne; imprinted with the Union Jack and the French tricolor, the cards extended a ''fraternal salute'' to the residents below. By February of 1920 Instone had begun carrying paying passengers on its route, and not long afterward the line earned a special place in aeronautical history when it put its pilots into uniform. As a maritime firm, Instone chose the traditional navy blue, a color that would become a standard for commercial flight officers all over the world.

All the pioneering airlines were dogged by breakdowns and other mishaps. One Handley Page pilot, Gordon Olley, claimed that he made 17 forced landings on a single flight from London to Paris; somehow he was able to find an open field whenever he had to come down. At Aircraft Transport and Travel, George Holt-Thomas called such unscheduled touchdowns ''involuntary descents,'' and he urged the establishment of a series of emergency landing fields every 10 miles along the land portion of the London-to-Paris route. But nothing ever came of the idea, and airliners continued to make emergency landings in bumpy meadows and wheat fields.

The primitive nature of navigational aids and weather reporting was among the chief reasons for the frequency of involuntary descents. London-bound pilots passing over the airfield at Lympne, near the English coast, got their information about visibility and wind direction over southern England by peering down at the field, where canvas strips were laid out in prearranged patterns. In time, the vagaries of the weather became a source of fun among the fliers, who would sometimes issue comic reports calling attention to such conditions as ''squaggy around Beauvais.'' Another notice stated that ''the cloud height given in yesterday's forecast as 3,000 meters should read 300 feet.''

England's renowned fog was no joke, however, and it confounded nearly everyone. Groping his way toward London one day, William Armstrong was skimming so close to the ground that he suddenly realized he was passing alongside a church steeple. The resourceful Gordon Olley found a way to beat the fog when he noticed that express trains hurtling through the gray curtain would disturb the air sufficiently to leave a visible furrow, which he could follow toward London. On one occasion he arrived over London's Croydon airport—opened to civilian traffic in 1920—to find the field totally socked in with only the tip of the control tower and a few nearby buildings visible. Using these to get his bearings and calling to mind the airfield's general layout, he very gingerly set the plane down in the pea-soup fog. Then he cut his en-

Flying high in style but low on comfort

"Only a contortionist could get into the front seat," complained a British airline pilot, describing the accommodations on a two-passenger plane he flew in 1919. "The comparative roominess of the back seat was offset by the gale of wind rushing around the whole time."

Such discomforts were typical of passenger aircraft in the early years following World War I. Fitted with lightweight wicker armchairs and overhead luggage nets, these planes offered a travel experience similar to that on an early bus: Passengers enjoyed the dignity of a seat but suffered noise, vibration, extreme temperatures and a bumpy ride.

While these crude carriers attracted enough business in remote areas where land transport was irregular and primitive, Europe's international routes had to lure customers from less expensive and more comfortable railways and passenger ships. To compete, many airlines fitted out their passenger cabins as airborne capsules of luxury and elegance.

Though the trimmings served mainly to distract passengers from their discomfort—there was little improvement in such matters as soundproofing and heating until later—air travel achieved in the 1920s a sumptuous style that has been unequaled since.

Adapted to civilian use, a French Farman Goliath bomber sports an after cabin furnished in Pullman-car style. A similar cabin was located in the front bomb bay.

Though the accommodations are spare, paintings grace the arched walls and lend elegance to a 1920 Vickers Vimy—a favorite with Britain's Instone Air Line.

The passenger cabin of a Fokker F.III—introduced by KLM in 1921—appears as stately and spacious as a lounge in a prestigious club. The pilot, however, still suffered the rigors of an open cockpit.

Decorative tile walls and ornate accessories distinguish this 1920 Caudron C.25 lavatory. Though many planes had washrooms, most were more primitive.

Built by the Deutsche Flugzeugwerke in Leipzig in 1919 and advertised as an air "limousine," this plane offered extravagant comfort with its upholstered interior.

gine and waited as airport officials groped through the fog to find him.

Most air travelers took such misadventures in stride. Olley recalled a time when he flew through a winter storm, his plane bucking and plummeting, ice forming on the wings. Unable to see his single passenger, who was in the cabin behind him, Olley assumed the man was petrified by fear. Then the small sliding door from the cabin was opened and a hand reached through it, offering Olley a sandwich.

Satisfied as they may have been, passengers were nevertheless not plentiful enough to make operations profitable, as the airlines learned to their chagrin. All of the pioneer lines lost money, and in Britain, at least, there were no subsidies available from the government. Winston Churchill, the Secretary of State for Air, had decreed that his country's struggling civil aviation industry "must fly by itself; the Government cannot possibly hold it up in the air." But the competitive French, who had begun regular flights to London in the fall of 1919, were enjoying generous subsidies from their government, which viewed the maintaining of cross-Channel flights as a matter of national honor.

In 1920 the French staggered their British rivals by cutting air fares on the Paris-to-London route. It was too much for George Holt-Thomas. By the end of the year he had sold out to a new organization, Daimler Airway. (His managing director, the irrepressible Sefton Brancker, continued to be an outspoken champion of commercial air travel and in 1922 was named the Air Ministry's Director-General of Civil Aviation.) But all of the British lines suspended service early in 1921, resuming in the spring only when the government relented and offered modest subsidies to help them meet their expenses.

Daimler quickly made a name for itself. Striving for efficiency, the company utilized its aircraft more intensively than did the other lines, and there were many occasions when all of its seven planes were in the air at once. Daimler also introduced the revolutionary notion that passengers might welcome someone to see to their comfort while they were in the air; in 1922 it hired three 14-year-old cabin boys, dressed them in the style of hotel bellboys and sent them aloft on key flights. Food and drink were not served aboard the planes, so the youngsters were more ornamental than useful. But their employment would soon lead to the use of adult stewards—and eventually to stewardesses, first introduced in the United States.

By 1923 British airline operators had widened their service by flying to such European cities as Amsterdam, Brussels and Cologne, and were compiling a record remarkably free of accidents. The lines thrived on publicity and on public-relations stunts that called attention to the wonders of air travel. School children flocked to the airfield at Croydon for guided tours. Instone Air Line offered brief demonstration flights for just five shillings; on one Sunday afternoon nearly 400 people went aloft, many for the first time in their lives.

Newspaper reporters, who might sing the praises of air travel to the public, were especially prized as passengers, and most of the airlines staged periodic flights for members of the press. It sometimes required a good deal of imagination to manage such a trip. Once, Handley Page's general manager, George Woods Humphery, learned that the well-known American writer and lecturer Lowell Thomas was interested in flying from England to Germany. Woods Humphery pulled out all the stops to ensure royal treatment for the distinguished traveler. Then at the last minute he discovered that Thomas would be the only passenger on board the plane.

Knowing that a bank of empty seats would hardly impress the visiting American with the popularity of the recently inaugurated service, Woods Humphery quickly arranged for airline employees to pose as passengers on the flight. The plan went smoothly until the plane reached its destination and the bogus passengers were enthusiastically greeted by their fellow airline staffers on the ground, who had not been tipped off to the ruse.

Despite their route expansion and their sometimes heroic efforts to gain favorable publicity, none of the British airlines were making much money. Clearly there were too many airlines for the available passengers. But a solution was at hand. A number of Britain's political leaders had argued persuasively that the Empire should link its far-flung outposts by air and that a single airline could do the job more effectively than several. It was therefore resolved to combine all the separate lines into a single organization, handsomely backed by the government, to serve as "the chosen instrument of the state for the development of air transport on a commercial basis." The resulting airline, which came into being in 1924, was tentatively named British Aircraft Transport Service, but George Woods Humphery observed that its initials—BATS—might convey an unfortunate impression of the proposed Empire-wide aerial enterprise. A better name, he suggested, would be the resounding Imperial Airways.

Woods Humphery's proposal for a name change was accepted. But his appointment as general manager of the newly formed line was opposed by the company's pilots, who strongly objected to his insistence that they follow rigid timetables. The pilots also were dissatisfied with their proposed pay schedules, and they declined to fly. Imperial Airways Ltd., scheduled to begin operations on April 1, 1924, spent most of its first month with all its planes on the ground.

To help settle the dispute, Woods Humphery chose H. G. Brackley—a former colleague at Handley Page Transport—to serve as Imperial's air superintendent and represent the pilots' interests. Brackley, known as Brackles, was himself an experienced flier and had the full confidence of both management and the disaffected pilots. He deftly ironed out the differences between the two sides, and by early May Imperial airliners were winging across the English Channel to Paris. Service to other European cities was soon added, and plans were under way to make Imperial Airways a truly Empire-wide operation.

Sir Alan Cobham's pensive gaze and well-thumbed navigation maps reflect the methodical approach he used on his pioneering flights to the far corners of the British Empire. King George V rewarded his efforts by making him a knight in 1926, when the flier was just 32 years old.

The first steps toward building such an airline had already been taken. Shortly after World War I, Britain had begun connecting its Middle Eastern outposts by air, and had set the RAF to flying straight across the desert between Cairo and Baghdad, carrying both military and civilian mail. The Baghdad airmail was to become the keystone of a vast airline network, but flying over the desert presented a number of problems not encountered in populous Western Europe. The area was largely unmapped and offered few landmarks that could guide a pilot. To solve this problem the British ran automobiles along the route to create a track that pilots could follow; in stretches where the track was difficult to spot, a tractor plowed a deep furrow that was plainly visible from the air. Because the Vickers biplanes used on the route were subject to frequent breakdowns, a backup craft usually accompanied each mailplane.

The pilots were in awe of what one British flier called the "mysterious fascination" of the open desert. "It seems to be a land with no ending," he explained, "and it has an unreal atmospheric quality comparable with the sky." Later, after the RAF had begun night flying, the same pilot wrote: "It is lovely flying cross-country on a moonlight night, all black, grey, green and silver; the quiet stars, and the ghostly desert, and the rivers with the faint golden glimmer of the moon on them, shining on some distant reach." But the desert was often treacherous. Dust storms could whip up without warning, destroying visibility and creating vicious winds. Even on relatively calm nights planes forced down in the desert had to be staked to the sands lest they blow over. Hot downdrafts could slam a plane into the ground in the middle of takeoff.

Despite such difficulties, British aviation authorities were considering extensions of the Middle Eastern operation, and in November of 1924 Director-General of Civil Aviation Brancker set out to survey an air route to India. For Brancker, the flight was the first step toward the realization of a years-old dream; as early as 1919, he had written of his belief that "aviation will be the greatest factor in linking up our world-wide Empire."

Brancker's pilot on the India expedition was Alan Cobham, a 30-year-old former barnstormer with a taste for long-distance flying. It was an eventful trip. The four-passenger de Havilland transport went in on its nose during a landing near Baghdad; it was quickly repaired. Brancker caught pneumonia in Calcutta, but he recovered and went on to his last stop, Rangoon, Burma, then a part of British India.

On the return flight, Cobham ran into a severe winter storm in Germany and was forced to land in a snow-covered field from which no takeoff was possible. Undismayed, Cobham and Brancker—together with their mechanic and some helpful German policemen—dismantled the plane. Then they loaded the parts onto trucks and drove 50 miles to an airfield outside Stuttgart, where they reassembled the craft and took off for London. Back home, Brancker submitted an optimistic report to his colleagues. "Generally speaking," he concluded, "the route between London and Rangoon is an extremely easy one for operation. I believe, therefore, that an aeroplane service along this route will fly with extraordinary regularity."

For political reasons, British planes were denied the use of some European airfields that were vital to regular commercial crossings of the Continent. But the first small step toward Brancker's grandiose goal was taken in late 1926 when Imperial Airways took over the RAF's route from Cairo to Baghdad and quickly extended it southeast to the Persian Gulf port city of Basra.

The three-engined, seven-passenger de Havilland aircraft that plied this pioneering desert air lane were more reliable than their predecessors, but they lacked the range to cross the entire 1,100-mile route in a single hop. And fuel supplies frequently dwindled sharply as the planes bucked prevailing head winds on the westward leg of the journey. It was simple enough to set out emergency caches of fuel at strategic spots along the way, but it was another matter to contend with nomadic Arabs who lived along the route. The Arabs were friendly enough, but they

kept stealing the fuel cans—not for the gasoline but for use as water containers and cooking utensils. When the British put their fuel in locked underground tanks, the Arabs used the locks for target practice. Stronger, hidden locks were substituted; pilots kept forgetting the keys. Finally the tanks were given the same locks as the airplane cabin doors, and the problem was solved.

With the cooperation of the government of Iraq, Imperial Airways built an overnight way station in mid-desert. The fortress-like hotel offered relatively comfortable accommodations, but passengers sometimes had to make do in rougher surroundings. One planeload, downed at dusk in the wilds, had to spend the night in an abandoned desert outpost. When they began to get cold, the pilot observed that many camels had been in the vicinity and suggested that his passengers might collect dried camel dung in their hats to use for fuel. The adventuresome air travelers took to the task with good humor, and soon they had a fire blazing merrily. Some months later the passengers met for a reunion dinner at a London restaurant and sent the pilot a menu signed "From the Camel Dung-Burners Club."

By 1929, Imperial had extended its Middle East service to Karachi, at that time a part of India. But the India route linked only a part of Britain's far-flung overseas possessions. Another axis of empire ran south from Cairo through the heart of Africa to the Cape of Good Hope. Any air

High and dry on a litter borne by local tribesmen, Alan Cobham is carried ashore after landing his seaplane in a tropical lagoon on the Malay coast in 1926. Cobham went on to Australia before returning to England, completing the 28,000-mile round trip in just a little more than three months.

route over such forbidding territory promised difficulties far different from those faced in the desert. Landing spots cleared from the jungle quickly became jungle again if they were not zealously maintained; and some of the African peoples were less than happy to have their privacy disrupted by airborne Europeans.

Alan Cobham was one pilot who relished such challenges. In the summer of 1925, fresh from his survey flight to India with Sefton Brancker, Cobham had begun planning a flight from London to Cape Town, South Africa. After arranging for landing sites and supplies along the way, Cobham set out from London on November 16, accompanied by the same mechanic who had flown with him to India and by a movie cameraman who was to record the expedition on film. Forty-five stops and 17,000 miles later, Cobham arrived safely home on March 13, 1926, to report that commercial air service to the tip of Africa would indeed be feasible. Yet it was not until 1932, after several years of building intermediate landing fields and radio stations, that Imperial Airways launched weekly service between London and Cape Town.

Cobham conducted yet another of his surveys later in 1926, this time flying across the Middle East and Southeast Asia all the way to Australia in a de Havilland that had been modified to serve as a seaplane. Near Baghdad an Arab hunter shot at his plane and fatally wounded his mechanic. Cobham found a new helper and continued on. Once, his plane was damaged during mooring, and after being repaired was damaged again when Cobham tried to take off. But he patched it up once more and kept going. Later, he was forced down by monsoon rains. When he reached Sydney, Australia, he was greeted by a tumultuous crowd of 60,000, and the multitude awaiting him in Melbourne a few days later was more than twice that size.

Australia was a land made for aviation: It was huge, sparsely populated and equipped with only the most meager road and railway systems. A number of small airlines were already in operation there, the most successful being the Queensland and Northern Territory Aerial Services, founded in 1920 by two World War I fliers and known, from its initials, as Qantas (pages 33-36). But aerial links with the rest of the world would be a long time coming, largely because of rivalries between the Australians and the English. Negotiations aimed at setting up some kind of cooperative intercontinental service did not get under way until 1930, and through service all the way from London to Brisbane, with the last leg operated by a jointly owned Imperial-Qantas company, finally was offered in 1935. At about the same time, Imperial was able to clear away political obstructions to stopovers in Europe and provide air access to the entire Empire.

By then Imperial was serving many of its long-distance routes with the Handley Page H.P.42, a massive four-engined biplane. The ultimate in elegance, the H.P.42 had a fuselage nearly as long and wide as a Pullman car and fully as comfortable, with wall-to-wall carpeting and a stand-up bar. Stewards served seven-course meals at tables that were

Alan Cobham soars past the Houses of Parliament as Londoners on board boats on the Thames greet his return from Australia in October 1926.

set up between facing seats. Large windows provided an ample view, and the cabin was partially soundproofed, a welcome innovation. The craft was exceedingly slow—pilots joked that it had "built-in head winds," and that trains could overtake it—but it was uncommonly safe, with a landing speed of only 50 miles per hour.

Imperial Airways had patriotically equipped the new planes with a specially designed flag called the British Civil Air Ensign, light blue with a dark blue cross, and a Union Jack in the corner. The flag was to be flown from a small staff on the fuselage only while the aircraft was loading, though crewmen sometimes forgot to bring it in before takeoff. Away the plane would roar, climbing sedately into the air as the slip stream bent the flagstaff almost horizontal. Someone in the control tower would notice and radio the plane: "Your flag." A hatch would open and a hand would reach out to rescue the wind-whipped ensign.

Soon other airlines were sporting flags, too, and by the late 1920s and early 1930s airfields abounded with the insignia of many nations. One of Imperial's strongest competitors, particularly on the demanding Far Eastern route, was KLM, whose initials stand for Koninklijke Luchtvaart Maatschappij, or Royal Air Traffic Company. The brain child of an energetic young Dutch aviator named Albert Plesman, the line had been founded in the autumn of 1919, not long after Plesman had organized a highly successful air show that impressed his countrymen with aviation's commercial potential. The new Dutch airline was financed by a number of wealthy Amsterdam businessmen and made its first flights—in British-built de Havilland D.H.16s—between Amsterdam and London in the spring of 1920.

Plesman was a strong-willed, opinionated executive who ran his operation with a firm hand. Like so many other pioneers, however, he was also a visionary, proclaiming that air travel was infinitely promising because the sky itself was infinite. He was soon buying planes from his countryman, the renowned designer Anthony Fokker, and flying to a number of European cities. But his eye was on the Netherlands' distant colonial holdings in the East Indies, and as early as 1924 he dispatched one of his pilots on an exploratory flight all the way to Java. This was about the time that Cobham and Brancker were setting out for Rangoon, and Plesman kept KLM moving in step with, or slightly ahead of, the British all the way to the East. By 1930 he had inaugurated weekly service between Amsterdam and Batavia, then capital of the Dutch East Indies, now Djakarta, Indonesia.

French airline operators had also been competing with the British, most directly for the Paris-to-London trade. The first serious French entry on this route had gotten under way in September 1919, when Lignes Aériennes Farman—Farman Air Lines—started regular service between the two capital cities. Founded by the three Farman brothers, Dick, Henry and Maurice—who had manufactured military aircraft during the War—the line was equipped at first with twin-engined Far-

Groundwork for an airline down under

Planning an air race to promote aviation, the Australian government in 1919 commissioned two pilots to drive across the outback exploring a route. The race's purpose was fulfilled even before it began: The trek itself inspired the surveyors, Hudson Fysh and P. J. McGinness, to found an Australian airline.

In a Model T Ford loaded with provisions, spare parts and fuel, the surveyors crossed 1,354 miles of trackless terrain in 51 grueling days, conquering unbridged rivers, sandy wastes and many mechanical breakdowns. Convinced that an airline could thrive in this sparsely settled region where land travel was nearly impossible, Fysh and McGinness in 1920 founded the Queensland and Northern Territory Aerial Services Ltd., or Qantas—in time, Australia's biggest airline.

Hudson Fysh sketches a possible landing site near Cloncurry, Queensland, in 1919.

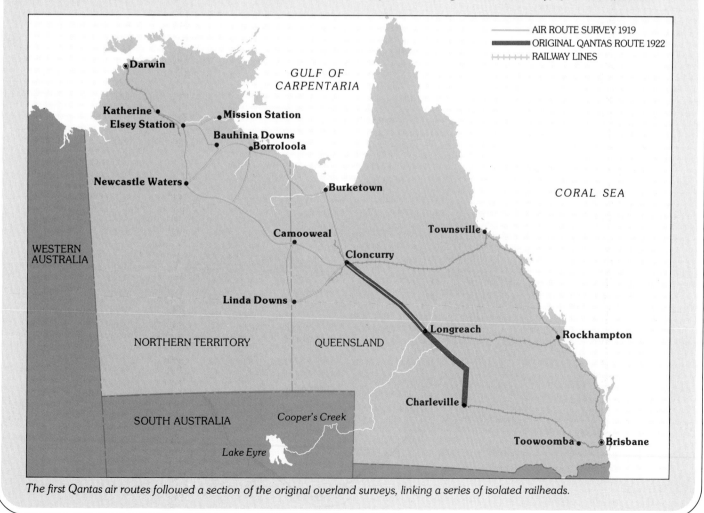

AIR ROUTE SURVEY 1919
ORIGINAL QANTAS ROUTE 1922
RAILWAY LINES

The first Qantas air routes followed a section of the original overland surveys, linking a series of isolated railheads.

Driver George Gorham (above) assesses the Ford's precarious position after the car's right rear wheel slipped over the edge of a deep gully hidden by high grass—one of many near disasters the expedition experienced. At right, helpful aborigines wrestle the Ford across the soft sand of a dry riverbed and, below, two horses drag it through the mud of a wet one.

Travel companions who accompanied Fysh on a return trip to Cloncurry in 1920 check their supply-laden Ford. The car suffered 41 tire punctures and traveled 150 miles on tires stuffed with grass.

Fysh and a mechanic stand near their plane at Luthrie Station—one stop on a tour they made in 1921, selling joy rides to local people.

A cart horse meets Australia's new air age at one of the first Qantas offices, established in Longreach late in 1921.

man Goliath bombers that had been converted to 12-passenger civilian transports. Soon a number of additional French companies were flying, along with Farman, to London and to other European cities, establishing a reputation for brisk in-flight service and, by the mid-1920s, for sumptuous cuisine.

Of far greater import for the future of French aviation were the heady plans of a Toulouse industrialist named Pierre Latécoère. A slender, cultivated, autocratic figure whose poor eyesight—like the Englishman Sefton Brancker, he wore a monocle—and reserved manner set him apart from the men who flew for him, Latécoère had manufactured munitions during the early part of World War I and had begun building military aircraft in 1917. Before long he had devised a grand scheme involving peaceful uses for his planes. In September 1918, as the War was drawing to a close, he proposed to develop a commercial air route leading from Toulouse, in the south of France, down through Spain and across the Mediterranean Sea to Morocco, then along Africa's desolate west coast to Senegal. From there, the proposed service would leap across the Atlantic to South America, where France had strong business interests.

After the Armistice was signed in November, Latécoère gathered to his factory airfield a band of wartime fliers and proceeded to create not only an aggressive, precedent-setting airline but a spirit of boldness and self-sacrifice that would earn the enterprise a special place in aviation history. To doubters who felt that flying had no role to play now that the War was over, he said flatly: "You believe aviation is finished; I believe it is just beginning."

Lignes Aériennes Latécoère—the Line, as it was soon called—would start by flying the mail across the Pyrenees to Barcelona. Among its first pilots was a 29-year-old war veteran whom Latécoère made general manager. His name was Didier Daurat. Stocky and impassive, but with piercing eyes that bespoke a deep intensity of purpose, Daurat was a tough disciplinarian whom the other aviators—and their families—treated with respect and learned not to cross. To all he was Monsieur Daurat. Once, the wife of a flier was standing near a hangar when she saw her husband's plane crash and burst into flames on takeoff. It was a heart-searing experience, yet she did not dare run to the crash scene lest she incur Daurat's displeasure—women, she knew, had no place on his airfield. His whole life seemed to revolve around flying, and pilots became accustomed to seeing his leather-jacketed figure already on the field when they arrived at dawn for early departures. Daurat would have been there for some time, warming up the engines and scanning the skies.

Flying battle-scarred Breguet biplanes that had been purchased as war surplus, Latécoère's men began air service to Spain in early 1919, first to Barcelona, then Alicante, then Málaga, on the southern coast. In September they made the jump to North Africa and began flying to Casablanca.

By the end of 1922 Latécoère felt confident enough to extend his trans-Mediterranean service to Algeria; he also dispatched a pilot to survey the route south from Casablanca through the western Sahara to Dakar, the proposed jumping-off-place for his flights across the Atlantic to South America. After careful preparation and a number of delicate talks with Spanish authorities in Madrid, flights along this route got under way in 1925.

In the hot, implacable desert the French pilots confronted the same difficulties that had beset the British east of Cairo, plus one other: the blue-veiled, nomadic tribesmen of Spain's Rio de Oro colony, just south of Morocco. The tribesmen were bitterly anti-European. Even the Spanish authorities could maintain control of the wind-swept territory only from well-manned forts.

The French laid out their landing fields next to these forts, but security was always tenuous. Away from the forts, when a Breguet's engine sputtered into silence and the plane was forced down in mid-desert, the pilots were highly vulnerable. Daurat ordered his planes to fly in pairs—if one was forced down, the other could land and act as a rescue plane. Through intermediaries he informed the hostile tribes that rewards would be paid if downed pilots were handed over unharmed. He also employed friendly Arabs to go along on some of the flights as interpreters to intercede, if necessary, with the desert warriors. Clad in turban and burnoose, the interpreter would curl up among the mailbags and go to sleep, ready to awaken if the plane jolted onto the sands and to convince his countrymen that French fliers were worth considerably more alive than dead.

For a while the technique worked: A sum would be agreed upon and the pilot quickly returned to his base. Then the situation took an ugly turn. In 1926, the exuberant Jean Mermoz, one of the Line's most venturesome pilots, was forced down by engine trouble in a sandstorm that screened him from his backup plane. Mermoz, who was alone in his plane, was quickly captured by a band of nomads who clapped him into a cage and hoisted him onto a camel. His captors then set off across the sands. For nine days Mermoz endured the camel's monotonous lurching under the blistering sun; then he was brought before a chieftain, who spat out his hatred for the French. But a ransom was arranged and Mermoz was freed.

Six months later a worse incident occurred. Two planes came down together in the wasteland and were attacked by tribesmen. The pilot and mechanic of one of the planes were killed instantly; the other pilot, flying alone, was badly wounded and, like Mermoz, was loaded onto a camel and taken away. He was ransomed a week later but died soon afterward in a Casablanca hospital.

Such incidents were critical setbacks, and the Line could not survive many more of them. But Latécoère and Daurat were able to continue their service across the desert, thanks in large part to the introduction of newer and more reliable planes that were less likely to break down in the

A Latécoère airliner swoops down over an exotic desert landscape in this French poster touting the company's France-to-Morocco mail service begun in 1919. Flown in a series of 10 short hops along the coasts of Spain and North Africa, the 875-mile trip took about 30 hours.

hot desert air. They were also aided by an impoverished young aristocrat named Antoine de Saint-Exupéry.

A man of great personal magnetism and charm, Saint-Exupéry was a gifted writer who had been enchanted by the beauty and excitement of flying and had become an accomplished pilot. Daurat had taken him on in late 1926 and assigned him to the Toulouse-Casablanca run. Then, with the desert nomads growing more and more disruptive, Daurat assigned the articulate, imaginative Saint-Exupéry to the trouble spot, putting him in charge of the way station at Cape Juby, on the Rio de Oro coast.

It was a masterly move. Saint-Exupéry set out to ingratiate himself with the hostile tribes and win their trust. In order to look more like the men he was dealing with, he grew a beard, allowed his skin to burn dark and frequently wore an old dressing gown that resembled a burnoose. So garbed, he often took a plane and ranged far and wide over the bleak desert, landing here and there to talk with Berber chiefs and reassure them of the Line's peaceful intent. His efforts paid off. Dangerous episodes declined—on many occasions Saint-Exupéry himself intervened to defuse troublesome incidents—and his outpost became an oasis of safety in the harsh desert. Jean Mermoz in particular delighted in stopping at Saint-Exupéry's way station, and the two men became fast friends.

Neither was to remain in Africa for long, however. Pierre Latécoère had maneuvered to set up an airmail service along the east coast of South America, hoping later to fulfill his grand design by connecting this segment with the African route. As early as 1924, Latécoère had sent emissaries to South America and won permission from the governments of Brazil, Uruguay and Argentina to start such a service. Later in the same year one of the Line's veteran pilots, Joseph Roig, arrived in South America to survey the coastal route between Rio de Janeiro and Buenos Aires, and work crews began clearing landing sites in the jungle.

But the farseeing Latécoère was about to be squeezed out as head of the expanding airline that he had so lovingly fashioned. To finance his move into South America he sought the aid of a wealthy French banker in Brazil, Marcel Bouilloux-Lafont. The banker gradually increased his investment until, in 1927, he took control of the Line; he even gave it a new name, Aéropostale. Latécoère returned regretfully to his aircraft manufacturing business in Toulouse.

Jean Mermoz arrived in South America late in 1927 to become Aéropostale's chief pilot, and service soon began between Natal and Buenos Aires with intermediate stops at such points as Rio de Janeiro and Montevideo. In March of 1928 postal service from Europe became possible when French naval vessels were assigned to carry the mail between Dakar and Natal. With their help a letter from Paris could reach Buenos Aires in eight and a half days, compared with more than two weeks by steamship alone.

Led by the bold and venturesome Mermoz, Aéropostale's pilots were soon speeding up delivery times by flying at night, guided by flares along the way. Then they crossed the forbidding Andes to Chile, on South America's west coast; they extended their routes from Buenos Aires into Paraguay to the north and into southern Argentina. Saint-Exupéry was put in charge of Argentine operations in 1929 and was soon surveying routes as far south as the Strait of Magellan. Aéropostale also pushed north from Brazil and operated a route in Venezuela. Only the South Atlantic—which had been crossed nonstop only once—remained to be spanned regularly by air, and in 1930 a powerful, long-range Latécoère seaplane was readied for the transoceanic leap. On May 12, Mermoz and two crewmen made an uneventful 1,890-mile nonstop mail flight from Dakar to Natal in 19 hours and 35 minutes.

With Mermoz' trailblazing flight, travel time from France to Buenos Aires could theoretically be reduced to a mere four days, and it seemed that Pierre Latécoère's old dream was about to be realized. But the Line soon fell upon hard times. The new seaplane was wrecked on its return flight; improved aircraft were ordered but they could not be made ready for several years. Meanwhile, Bouilloux-Lafont had mismanaged his airline and had overextended himself financially; in 1931 Aéropostale was all but bankrupt.

Mail pilot Jean Mermoz (right), whose exploits inspired Antoine de Saint-Exupéry's 1931 novel Night Flight, relaxes with mechanic Amédée Jayat at the Latécoère airline's Casablanca terminal in 1926. "In the pitch-black night," Saint-Exupéry wrote, "Mermoz would land by the faint glimmer of three gasoline flares."

The pilots were devastated by Aéropostale's virtual collapse. Daurat was dismissed as general manager, and Mermoz and the others carried on as best they could. Then in 1933 a number of French airlines, seeking to pool their resources and present a united front when negotiating with the government about routes and subsidies, joined together to form a single company. The resulting national airline, called Air France, included Aéropostale, the old Farman line and Air Orient, which was operating passenger service from Marseilles to Baghdad and flying the mail all the way to Saigon.

At first the new organization was disposed to abandon the South American routes that the Line had so painstakingly forged. Mermoz returned to Paris and pleaded tirelessly with Air France's top officials. You must not turn your back, his argument went, on what we have achieved. In the end the officials relented, and Air France would later acknowledge its strong debt to Latécoère and the bold aviators who had given the French international airline a firm foothold in Africa and in South America.

For all their trailblazing *esprit*, however, the pilots of the Line had not flown alone over the beaches, jungles and mountains of South America. From the start, they had faced stiff competition from an American line, Pan American Airways, and from a variety of enterprises controlled by France's traditional European rival, Germany.

The German air effort had come a long way since its first commercial flights of 1919. No nation took more enthusiastically to the skies during the postwar era. Ironically, the harsh surrender terms that were imposed at Versailles benefited the development of German civil aviation. Barred from building large aircraft of any kind, the Germans applied all their ingenuity to making small, efficient planes that were ideally suited for commercial uses.

The postwar German government, ineffectual in many other ways, avidly promoted aviation. Before the end of 1919 a number of small lines were operating out of Berlin; so many others were soon added that some kind of consolidation was needed. By 1925 the system was dominated by two large groups, one called Deutscher Aero Lloyd and controlled by one of Germany's major shipping companies, the other a Junkers combine directed by the aircraft manufacturer of the same name. Inefficient duplication of routes still existed, however, and in 1926 all the German airlines were placed under the umbrella of one government-backed concern, Deutsche Luft Hansa Aktiengesellschaft—known more simply as Luft Hansa.

This new organization continued to expand in an atmosphere of practicality and good cheer. Germans were encouraged to visit the flying fields, and Berlin's Tempelhof Airport, with its rooftop restaurant, was the picture of gaiety. Luft Hansa's fares were lower, mile for mile, than those of French and British airlines: The German line could afford this, because the state picked up 70 per cent of each flight's cost. In

1926, beacons were installed along the major air route between Berlin and Königsberg (now Kaliningrad, in the Soviet Union), and on May 1, 1926, night passenger flights—claimed by the Germans to be the first in the world—were initiated between the two cities. By 1928 the airline had equipped its planes with comfortable reclining seats and offered hot meals aloft.

Luft Hansa was reaching out beyond Germany's borders, too. As early as 1922 flights to Moscow had been offered in cooperation with a Soviet organization. Later on, service was inaugurated to Scandinavia, to Rome, to Paris and eventually all the way to Baghdad—where the Germans competed directly with Britain's Imperial Airways, as well as with Air France. By the middle 1930s Germany had developed the largest commercial aviation system in Europe.

German airline promoters had also looked for routes far beyond the confines of continental Europe and the Middle East. Possibilities seemed especially attractive in South America, where there were many German immigrants and business interests. But instead of operating their own airlines there, the Germans chose an indirect path, establishing locally based subsidiary companies that used German aircraft and were staffed with German personnel. The first such venture, known by its initials in Spanish as SCADTA, had been founded in Colombia as early as December 1919, although regularly scheduled service did not begin until 1921.

The largest and most significant of these subsidiary enterprises was the Kondor Syndikat, formed in 1924. Primarily a Brazilian operation, Kondor had begun by the late 1920s to operate routes up and down the South American continent, paralleling the one being flown by the French pilots of Aéropostale. But the Germans' main object, of course, was to set up a Europe-to-Rio de Janeiro line similar to the one the French were laboring to perfect.

Despite their acknowledged technical proficiency, however, the Germans had difficulty in developing a plane that could fly nonstop across the South Atlantic. In 1929 they demonstrated a mammoth flying boat known as Dornier Do X, but this ambitious aeronautical design failed dismally as a practical transoceanic airliner (pages 44-49).

To be sure, by the early 1930s Germany was providing glamorous and dependable Zeppelin service direct from Europe to South America. But dirigible flights were few in number and could be operated only in mild weather; heavier-than-air craft were needed to maintain regularly scheduled operations throughout the year. The Germans experimented for a while with various ship-plane combinations; then in 1933 they started to use an ingenious technique that served them well for a number of years. At strategic points along the South Atlantic route they stationed ships equipped for refueling operations and for catapulting aircraft into the air. A flying boat would land at the stern of a ship; it would then be hoisted aboard and trundled to a track at the bow. There it would be swiftly refueled, then flung aloft by catapult to con-

Planes crowding the passenger boarding area at Paris' Le Bourget airfield in 1936 include (clockwise from bottom left) a French Simoun mailplane, a Junkers Ju 52, a British Scylla biplane, a four-engined de Havilland D.H.86a, a big Italian Savoia S-74, a Swiss-Air DC-2 (center) and an Air France Wibault-Penhoet 28.

tinue the journey. The scheduled flight time from Berlin to Buenos Aires was reduced to just four or five days. By 1935 Lufthansa—as the German national airline had begun styling itself—was flying the South Atlantic route by night, reducing the Berlin-to-Rio de Janeiro flight time to three days.

As the 1930s advanced, much of the world was crisscrossed by airline routes. Russia, Italy, Poland, Sweden, Switzerland, Czechoslovakia and Japan were among the many nations that had joined the pioneers of Great Britain, France, the Netherlands and Germany in establishing commercial air networks. Most of these airlines were government-supported, and many of their services would be severely disrupted during the coming years of war, but the route systems that were established in the 1920s and 1930s would be the basis of a tremendous growth in postwar air travel. And the laggard United States had by now advanced far beyond the trailblazing but short-lived St. Petersburg-Tampa Airboat Line of 1914. Guided by a handful of hard-driving aviation entrepreneurs, America was becoming a worldwide leader in the peacetime exploitation of the air. ❦

World War I flying ace Friedrich Christiansen captained the giant Do X on its first transatlantic flight—an island-hopping junket from Lisbon, Portugal, to Natal, Brazil, in the spring of 1931.

An airborne colossus ahead of its time

In December 1926, Claude Dornier, a German designer of Zeppelins, unveiled plans for a passenger plane he hoped would render dirigibles — then the only kind of aircraft to make regularly scheduled Atlantic crossings — obsolete.

Dornier's daring creation, which he called the Do (for Dornier) X (for unknown quantity), was a huge flying boat with 12 engines and a 157-foot wingspan — by far the largest heavier-than-air flying machine the world had seen. Designed to carry about 70 passengers for more than a thousand miles without refueling, the Do X was immensely powerful. On its first test flight in July 1929, it leaped off the water before its pilot was ready; on another occasion it effortlessly carried 169 passengers. As well as being a technological marvel, the Do X was a flying pleasure dome with dining rooms, sleeping quarters and a central saloon 23 feet long carpeted with Oriental rugs.

To promote his plane, Dornier organized a gala air cruise to New York that would include stops all over Europe and South America. But a series of minor accidents and an endless stream of curious visitors waiting to see the plane at every stop threw it disastrously off schedule.

When the Do X finally reached New York 10 months after starting its journey, Dornier found that his plane had become a joke in the world press and that his financial backing was dwindling. Even after making the return trip in just six days, the Do X was considered an unrealistic venture. The plane never crossed the Atlantic again, and Dornier reluctantly donated it to a Berlin museum.

The giant Do X lifts off from the glassy water of Lake Constance, Switzerland, to begin its maiden flight to New York.

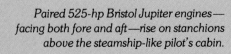

A bright-faced crowd of passengers
(perhaps including some of nine stowaways
who sneaked on board) crowd the Do X
on a test flight in October 1929.

Paired 525-hp Bristol Jupiter engines—
facing both fore and aft—rise on stanchions
above the steamship-like pilot's cabin.

Linen, crystal and plush upholstered
furniture grace the airplane's main saloon,
where passengers could take their meals
and play parlor games.

Octagonal crawl spaces lead through
the wing to the engines, enabling the crew
to make adjustments while in flight.

A flight engineer selects the correct
propeller speed for takeoff in November
1930, at the start of the trip to America.

Soaring high over the Rhine Valley on its way to Amsterdam, the Do X catches the glint of the setting sun on its wings.

2
America's young airlines: saved by the mail

Spring rains had saturated the Boston airport, a cindered field recently built on filled-in tidal land known as Commonwealth Flats. A traveler, businessman James Reddig, stepped off the trolley from East Boston and set off across the mire to look for the Colonial Air Transport ticket office. It was nowhere to be seen. Nor were there many planes—nor much of anything else indicating the presence of an airline. Reddig was somewhat puzzled. His flight to New York was part of a two-week passenger-carrying experiment that Colonial, a mail carrier, was conducting in the spring of 1927, and he had made his reservation just the day before.

As he was wondering what to do next, he heard someone shouting his name from a shanty that leaned up against a National Guard hangar. "Colonial's man slogged to meet me," Reddig recalled later, "shook my hand and seized my bag, and led me back through the thick mud to the shanty, which reeked of a coal-oil space heater. He shoved a mass of dirty engine parts along a bench fastened to the hangar wall and retrieved a battered typewriter from the floor. After wiping his hands on his coat, he racheted a Colonial letterhead, carbon and tissue into the machine and painfully finger-pecked my airline 'ticket,' following a sample tacked on the hangar wall. Pulling out his misspelled handiwork with a proud grin, he signed it with a flourish, took my $25, and carried my bag to the airplane."

Not long after the Fokker Trimotor was airborne, the pilot, dressed in a dinner jacket, white silk scarf and derby, appeared in the cabin for a chat. He was so garbed, he explained, because he was on his way to a party in New York. There was no copilot; the plane was being flown by a mechanic logging valuable flight time. Reddig was surprised to learn that although four passengers were aboard he was the only one paying to fly—the others were freeloading reporters—and that he represented the airline's first passenger revenue in 11 days.

At Hadley Field, near New Brunswick, New Jersey, where the flight terminated, Reddig got another surprise: There was no provision for ground transportation to New York. He hitched a ride in a mail truck to the railroad station in New Brunswick, where, he had been assured,

Passengers boarding a National Air Transport plane in the late 1920s pay their fares at a runway ticket office—hastily set up beneath a large umbrella—before squeezing into the cabin along with the mail.

New York-bound trains came through at least once an hour. Unfortunately, few of them bothered to stop at New Brunswick, and in the end it took Reddig longer to get from Hadley to New York than it had taken him to fly from Boston to Hadley.

In such haphazard, almost casual fashion, commercial passenger airlines were struggling into existence in the United States in the mid-1920s—when much of Europe was already covered by a network of air routes. Through the first half of the postwar decade, only one minor American passenger line had flourished for any length of time. That was Aeromarine West Indies Airways, formed in 1920 by the exotically named Inglis M. Uppercu after he had taken over a small airline that had been carrying mail over the 100-mile route between Key West, Florida, and Havana, Cuba.

Uppercu, a Manhattan Cadillac dealer who had also manufactured seaplanes for the United States Navy during World War I and operated an aerial sightseeing service in New York, soon added passengers to the Key West-Havana run and extended his service to Miami and the Bahamas as well. Guessing correctly that there were enough Prohibition-parched Americans to support regularly scheduled flights to areas where alcoholic beverages were served openly and for the asking, Uppercu soon began operating all the way from New York to Havana, picking up passengers in Atlantic City, New Jersey, and Beaufort, South Carolina, along the way. His airline—often referred to by thirsty travelers as the Highball Express—made money for several years. During the off-season summers of 1922 and 1923, the enterprising automobile dealer even shifted northward to offer services between Detroit and Cleveland, trimming a five-hour train trip to just 90 minutes' flying time.

Unfortunately for Uppercu, a pair of widely publicized accidents in the ocean off Florida caused a decline in passenger traffic. In one of the mishaps, a chartered flying boat belonging to another air-service operator was forced down by engine trouble; it bobbed for days in shark-infested waters, and the five passengers weakened and slipped one by one into the sea. The pilot, picked up at last by a passing ship, lived to tell a lurid tale that was printed on front pages throughout the nation. Soon afterward a similar disaster befell one of Uppercu's aircraft, with the loss of four lives.

In addition to souring the public on air travel, the accidents turned the financial community against investments in airline enterprises. "You cannot get one nickel for commercial flying," complained Uppercu, and in 1923 he shut down his airline.

Given the general unreliability of aircraft at the time and the lack of interest on the part of the government and the public, it could hardly have been otherwise. As the European experience had demonstrated, an airline could not exist for long without government support, but no subsidies were forthcoming from Washington. Most Americans remained skeptical about air travel; trains, while not as fast as planes, were

Jack Knight, who became a national hero after he completed the first night mail flight, part of a record-setting transcontinental airmail relay in 1921, sits at the controls of a de Havilland biplane. "I happened to be the man on the spot," he told reporters later, "but any of the rest of the fellows would have done what I did."

much safer. ("What's the use of getting there quicker," asked President Calvin Coolidge, "if you haven't got anything better to say when you arrive?") European governments had supported commercial aviation for reasons of national prestige, but in American politics "subsidy" was a dirty word. There were no such strong objections, however, to spending to improve an existing government service—such as carrying the mail. So it happened that organized air transport in the United States started with flying the mail. And the way the early airmail service developed provided the springboard that would enable American commercial aviation, by the late 1920s, to catch up with the Europeans and then to surpass them.

Congress had appropriated money as early as 1917 for a trial airmail run, and service between New York and Washington got under way in the spring of 1918. Flights were made by Army planes and pilots until August, when the Post Office began putting into service its own fleet of aircraft—a handful of Standard Aircraft Corporation biplanes at first, but later a large number of modified war-surplus de Havilland D.H.4 biplanes. Unfortunately, the planes were underpowered and mechanically fickle, and forced landings were frequent; they became even more frequent that winter, when Post Office officials tried and failed to introduce service from New York to Chicago.

Despite the hazards—three airmail pilots were killed in 1919, nine the following year—the Post Office kept extending its routes. By September 1920 the continent was spanned from New York to San Francisco, though flights took place only during daylight hours; at night, the mail was put on a train. Then in February of 1921, fearing that the economy-minded administration of incoming President Warren G. Harding might do away with the airmail service, the Post Office staged a dramatic demonstration of what it could do in the way of coast-to-coast speed. Flying by day and by night, a team of pilots carried the mail in relays from San Francisco to New York in a record-breaking 33 hours and 20 minutes.

The widely publicized flight convinced the new administration that the airmail should be not only continued but improved, and the government began installing beacons along the transcontinental airway. The first stretch to be marked was from Chicago to Cheyenne, Wyoming, with revolving beacons flashing into the night sky and with amply lighted emergency landing fields located every 25 to 30 miles along the way. By the middle of 1924 the lighted airway had been completed all the way from New York to San Francisco, and overnight service from New York to Chicago was introduced in the following year. The beacon system was a highly significant achievement, for nothing else like it existed anywhere. Night service in all other countries was sporadic at best, and would be for years. Civil aviation in the United States had in one quantum leap progressed technically beyond any in the world.

The Post Office planes, however, carried only mail, and as revenues increased, political pressure built up to turn the service over to private airline operators, who would labor under no such restriction. Oddly enough, such a move was spearheaded by the railroad interests, uneasy over the government's entry into the long-distance transport of mail. Representative Clyde Kelly of Pennsylvania, known as the "voice of the railway mail clerks," introduced in Congress a bill to put mail-carrying contracts up for competitive bidding. The Kelly Act, passed in 1925, left the transcontinental route to the Post Office. But the new law instructed the Post Office to enlist private contractors to fly mail over a number of feeder lines leading into the coast-to-coast trunk line, and bids were duly invited. The winners were a motley lot, some more enterprising and efficient than others, but all of them benefited from the Post Office's experience; some actually hired former government pilots. And when passenger carrying became feasible the resulting network of lines, after numerous permutations and additions, became the nucleus of the modern American airline industry.

The first such operator to get into the air was the automobile manufacturer Henry Ford, who already owned an airline of sorts. Always intrigued by new contraptions, Ford had been quietly exploring aviation's potential for a number of years; at one time, he had even given some thought to turning out airplanes by the same assembly-line methods that he used for his automobiles. Then an inventor named William B. Stout asked for Ford's financial backing in building an all-metal aircraft—a radical idea at a time when most planes were still built of fabric stretched over wooden frames. Ford, his son Edsel and a number of other Detroit businessmen came to Stout's aid, and Stout organized his own company to build a metal monoplane. Impressed with the plane's prospects, Ford bought Stout's firm in 1925, making it a division of the Ford Motor Company. Stout, more effective as a promoter than as an engineer, was soon dispatched on a lecture tour while Ford's own engineers refined his airplane design to create the famous Ford Trimotor. Known affectionately as the Tin Goose, the craft would become a mainstay of the airlines in the late 1920s.

Shortly before acquiring the Stout company, Ford had organized Ford Air Transport Service, which ferried spare parts between the company's plants. With the passage of the Kelly Act, Ford won contracts to carry the mail on the Detroit-Chicago and Detroit-Cleveland routes. The line flew briskly for more than three years, hauling cargo as well as mail and establishing a perfect safety record.

Stout, meanwhile, had continued his own pioneering. In the summer of 1926 he organized Stout Air Services to carry mail and passengers between Detroit and Grand Rapids but soon gave up his mail contract to concentrate on freight and passengers. In 1927 he dropped his Grand Rapids service in favor of a regular route to Cleveland. Then in 1928, Henry Ford decided that his company should stick to building planes and turned his airline routes over to Stout Air Services.

Although Stout had flown passengers from the outset, few other airlines followed suit. Passenger carrying required large and expensive

Unlikely father of the first airliner

On August 22, 1919, some 500 local citizens assembled on a farmer's field near Milwaukee, Wisconsin, skeptically eyeing an ungainly, box-tailed biplane that had been towed there by a team of horses. The plane's creator—an eccentric, 50-year-old former magazine publisher and aspiring aircraft manufacturer named Alfred W. Lawson—and a crew of four climbed into the cockpit, gunned the engines and roared aloft. Twenty minutes later they landed nearby, having completed the maiden flight of the world's first true passenger airliner.

The Lawson C-2 was the only large, multiengined plane of its day expressly built to transport people instead of mail or bombs. Powered by two 400-hp Liberty engines, it could carry 26 passengers more than 400 miles. Lawson quickly set out on a well-publicized cross-country tour in the prototype but failed to attract any buyers: Surplus military aircraft from World War I were available for less than half of the C-2's $50,000 cost.

Undaunted, Lawson built another, still larger transport, a jumbo three-engined airliner capable of carrying 34 passengers and 6,000 pounds of mail. But the new plane crashed during its first test flight, and Lawson's overextended company soon followed suit.

Admitting defeat, Lawson withdrew from aviation entirely and put his talents to work in a variety of successful get-rich-quick schemes before finally founding an unlikely religious cult—Lawsonomy—dedicated, among other aims, to preserving his memory as the father of the first commercial airliner.

Visionary Alfred W. Lawson exhibits determination in this 1927 portrait. He claimed to have coined the term "aircraft" while he was the publisher of Fly, America's first popular aviation magazine.

A 1920 poster extolling the safety record of the C-2 airliner features a picture of the plane showing its completely enclosed passenger cabin and boxlike tail assembly.

LAWSON CREATOR OF THE AIRLINER

THERE HAS NEVER BEEN A PERSON HURT IN A LAWSON AIRPLANE

FACTS ARE BETTER THAN FANCIES

HERE IS A FACT — AN ACTUAL PHOTOGRAPH OF THE GREAT 26 PASSENGER CARRYING LAWSON AIRLINER PASSING OVER NEW YORK HARBOR ON ITS 2500 MILE HISTORY MAKING TRIP FROM MILWAUKEE TO WASHINGTON AND RETURN.

LAWSON AIRLINE COMPANY - MILWAUKEE, WISCONSIN, U. S. A.

planes that were beyond the means of most of the lines; besides, mail was where the money was. In 1926 airlines were paid three dollars per pound for flying the mail a thousand miles; to take in as much for carrying a 150-pound passenger as for hauling an equivalent weight in airmail, a line would have had to charge a prohibitive $450 per ticket. Colonial Air Transport, the winner of the Boston-to-New York contract, carried no passengers for almost a year before chancing the two-week experiment during which James Reddig flew with the tuxedo-clad pilot and the reporters; not for more than another year did the airline try again to transport passengers. The contractor for St. Louis-Chicago, Robertson Aircraft Corporation, made no effort to get into passenger-carrying operations; the line is chiefly remembered for having hired as its head pilot a quiet, lanky young former barnstormer named Charles A. Lindbergh, who flew the mail in Robertson's D.H.4 biplanes for nearly six months before deciding to stake his future on a nonstop solo flight across the Atlantic Ocean.

In the western United States, passenger business seemed to offer more opportunities, partly because of the greater distances between major cities. One of the most vigorous of the new air carriers in that part of the country was Western Air Express, founded by some leading Los Angeles citizens who were indignant at San Francisco's designation as the West Coast terminus of the nation's sole transcontinental airmail route. Their ambitions were embodied in the man they chose as president, Harris M. Hanshue, a gravel-voiced, 40-year-old former automobile racer whose genial, if autocratic, ways had earned him the nickname of Pop. The aggressive and inventive Hanshue captured the Los Angeles-to-Salt Lake City airmail contract and then set about hiring a skilled nucleus of veteran military pilots. Using Douglas M-2 biplanes similar to the craft that the Post Office had only recently adopted to replace its worn-out de Havillands, Western started operating on April 17, 1926, thus earning the right in later years—after it had taken the name Western Airlines—to bill itself as the oldest surviving scheduled air carrier in the nation.

Pop Hanshue was unstinting in his promotion of Western's airmail service. "Fly Your Mail!" blared one company brochure. "Constant! Direct! Daily!" But his pilots were cautioned to cruise at low speed to save gas and baby the engines. By dint of such tactics, and because the route was a bonanza—within six months Los Angeles was sending or receiving 40 per cent of all airmail in the United States—Western quickly began earning a profit, the first of the new airlines to do so from the start. Meanwhile, just a month after beginning operations, Hanshue was carrying his first paying passengers. Only a trickle at first, passenger volume soon increased dramatically: In 1929, Western carried nearly 22,000 passengers—three times as many as it had flown during all of the previous three years.

Travel on a Western airliner was primitive at best. A passenger was outfitted in coveralls, helmet and goggles, handed a box lunch, strapped into a parachute harness and perched on a folding seat atop the mail sacks in the plane's forward compartment. There was far too much noise for conversation, but pilots sometimes took the time to scribble explanatory messages that were forerunners of a later era's chatty amplified announcements. A woman passenger saved hers; her pilot was something of a comedian. "We climb up over the Mormon Range now," read one note. "Cedar City up against mountains on the left. Don't know if you can see it or not. We get 10,000 feet again to go over this range. It is the highest and roughest spot on this trip. If you feel a bump in a few minutes you will know that you have crossed the Utah-Nevada line. If you get bumped out, don't forget to pull ripcord in chute and if it doesn't work bring it back. They are guaranteed."

Because it served Hollywood, Western transported its share of movie celebrities. One day pilot Fred Kelly was lucky enough to fly the starlet Bebe Daniels down from Salt Lake City. Such good fortune was too great not to share, and as Kelly passed pilot Charles "Jimmy" James, who was on the northbound flight out of Los Angeles, he waggled his wings in the prearranged signal to land. Mystified, James circled back and set down near Kelly on the desert, where he was overjoyed to be introduced to the glamorous passenger. They chatted for some time, then took off and went their separate ways. In Los Angeles, Kelly was asked by his supervisor, operations chief Corliss Moseley, why he had been so late in arriving. "Head winds," replied Kelly. Just then the phone rang. It was James, calling from Salt Lake City to report that he, too, had arrived late. Moseley asked him the same question. "Head winds," responded James.

Somewhat similar to Pop Hanshue's line, but not so large or tightly run, was Varney Air Lines, which fed into the transcontinental trunk line at Salt Lake City from the northwest. Walter T. Varney was a resourceful ex-World War I flier who had set up a flying school in the San Francisco area and operated an air-ferry service across San Francisco Bay. When he heard of the routes up for bids under the Kelly Act he noted one stretching from Elko, Nevada, to Pasco, Washington, by way of Boise, Idaho. Figuring that no one else would want to fly between such unlikely places he put in a bid—and sure enough, it was the only one submitted. Varney started modestly, persuading a flight instructor, three student pilots and four mechanics from his school to make up the operating staff. Then he added a bookkeeper and a promoter to drum up the public's interest in airmail.

It was not easy to fly in the rarefied mountain atmosphere, and Varney had the poor luck to start out with underpowered Swallow biplanes that were a challenge to put into the air at all. One technique that is said to have worked on occasion involved two saplings laid on the runway, one immediately in front of the plane's wheels as it prepared for takeoff and the other a couple of hundred yards down the strip. The first would act as a brake: The pilot could gun his engine almost to full throttle before the plane jumped the sapling and roared off, rolling

An early-morning crowd jams Vail Field in Los Angeles to see off the first Western Air Express mail flight, to Salt Lake City, on April 17, 1926.

Pop Hanshue (second from right) weighs Western's first 256 pounds of mail.

Two passengers, wearing helmets and goggles, weigh in on May 23, 1926.

fast. When it hit the second sapling the plane would bounce from the ground and become airborne.

Varney eventually acquired some stronger and faster Stearman aircraft, and business picked up, particularly around Christmas time, when there were so many mailbags to carry that some had to be tied to the wing struts. Then the Post Office allowed him to drop Elko from his route and to fly from Boise directly to Salt Lake City; later, he was permitted to go in the other direction, from Pasco all the way to Spokane and Seattle. Suddenly Varney had control of the quickest air route between the Pacific Northwest and points east.

But the choicest of the feeder routes ran up the Pacific coast from Los Angeles via San Francisco to Seattle. There the mail contract had been won by an enterprising promoter named Vern C. Gorst, a veteran of the Klondike gold rush, who had been operating a number of bus lines in the coastal states. Gorst was a longtime aviation enthusiast, and when he learned of the Kelly Act in late 1925 he yearned to take advantage of it. While addressing a group of bus-company managers he proposed that they pool their resources and start an airline. Enough money was raised to pay for a survey, and Gorst hired a stunt pilot to fly him from San Francisco north to the Canadian border and back again. He reported to his associates that transporting the mail along the coast by airplane was perfectly feasible.

The survey flight had cost only $48.25 for gas and oil, but now Gorst needed to raise big money—as a mail-contract bidder, he would be required to demonstrate a solid financial base. Traveling from city to city up and down the West Coast, he peddled $175,000 worth of stock and hired as pilots some barnstormers who were willing to take a portion of their wages in additional stock certificates. When bids on the coastal mail contract were opened, Gorst had prevailed. He called his new corporation Pacific Air Transport.

Gorst and his pilots moved quickly to persuade towns along the route to lay out airfields. As aids for nighttime flying he bought some old marine searchlights and installed them as mountaintop beacons. And he ordered some promising new monoplanes designed by T. Claude Ryan of San Diego. But troubles arose soon after Pacific Air started its scheduled operations in September 1926. Three pilots lost their lives in crashes; mail revenue was never sufficient to pay all the bills, and Gorst took to paying not only his pilots but fuel companies and other suppliers in Pacific Air Transport stock.

Then the hard-pressed Gorst went one day to the main office of the Wells Fargo Bank in San Francisco to see about a loan. It was the lunch hour, and most of the officers were out. But a short and intent young man named William A. Patterson, recently promoted to assistant vice president, talked to him and asked the purpose of the loan. Gorst explained that he wanted the money to retrieve the engine of a plane that had crashed and sunk in San Francisco Bay. Under questioning from Patterson, Gorst conceded that the engine had probably been

Maude Campbell, the first woman to fly on Western Air Express, clutches a spray of gladioluses after arriving in Los Angeles in 1926. Another female traveler, actress Bebe Daniels, stands with pilot Fred Kelly before a 1927 flight during which Kelly made an unscheduled landing to introduce his passenger to a fellow pilot.

ruined by the salt water, and the two men agreed that it would not be worth salvaging after all. But the banker pressed Gorst for details about his struggling airline, and Gorst invited him out to the company's airfield for a first-hand look. Patterson liked what he saw and decided to lend $5,000 to Pacific Air—not to buy the questionable engine but to meet general expenses.

Wells Fargo's president, Frederick Lipman, did not think very much of the idea. The airline business, he told his young subordinate, would never amount to much. But Patterson stuck to his guns, though he agreed to keep an especially close eye on Pacific Air Transport lest the company continue its seat-of-the-pants ways and default on the loan. The young bank executive was soon spending much of his spare time helping Gorst put the line on a more businesslike footing, and the operation began to approach solvency.

It was hardly surprising that Patterson had acted so decisively. He was only 27 at the time, but he had already had considerable experience with the ways of the world. Born in Hawaii, where his father managed a sugar plantation, Patterson was only seven when his father died. His mother struggled for six years to make a living, then moved to San Francisco in search of better opportunities, leaving her 13-year-old son behind at a military school in the islands. Patterson hated the school. He ran away once, but was caught and returned. Then he ran away again, this time for good. He signed on as a cabin boy on an oceangoing schooner and worked his way to the American mainland, enduring seasickness for the entire 23-day passage.

Back with his mother again, he took jobs delivering groceries and newspapers until he graduated from grammar school; then he answered an advertisement and was taken on as an office boy by Wells Fargo. He was just 15. His fellow employees took an immediate liking to

him, for he was both extroverted and quick-thinking; one of them urged him to take night courses to improve himself. Friends at the boarding-house where he moved after his mother's remarriage also saw room for improvement: They changed his nickname from Willie to Pat.

Like many other young men of the time, Pat Patterson became enchanted with airplanes. He once spent two weeks' wages on a flight over San Francisco Bay in an old crate through whose floorboards he got a good view of the water. His involvement with Vern Gorst in early 1927 was a dream come true. Thanks to Patterson's watchfulness, Gorst's determination and the reliable performance of the Ryan mail-planes, Pacific Air Transport seemed to be on its way to becoming a successful concern.

Even so, Gorst was still strapped for cash and was vulnerable to any takeover threat. Later in 1927 he was approached by Western Air's Pop Hanshue, who coveted the lucrative coastal mail route and offered to buy Gorst's controlling stock in Pacific Air Transport to acquire it. But Patterson advised against the deal, pointing out that it would shortchange too many innocent shareholders—among them the trusting pilots who had been paid in stock—and Gorst turned down Hanshue's proposal. But when another possibility opened up soon afterward, Patterson was in favor of selling the entire organization, this time to the expanding Boeing aviation empire.

An old-fashioned stagecoach adds a touch of nostalgia to the festivities marking the takeoff of Varney Air Lines' first mail flight from Pasco, Washington, in 1926. The coach, which once carried mail between Pasco and Spokane, is drawn up next to the Swallow biplane that was about to leave for Boise, Idaho, and Elko, Nevada.

Pacific Air Transport president Vern C. Gorst (left) and aircraft manufacturer T. Claude Ryan radiate confidence on arriving in Seattle after a survey flight from San Francisco in March 1926. The line's Ryan-built mailplanes began scheduled service along the Northwest Pacific coast the following September.

William E. Boeing was known primarily as a plane builder, but his Seattle-based company was also heavily involved in airline operations. Boeing had shown few early signs that he would one day head a major aeronautical enterprise: He had first become fascinated by aircraft simply because they were fun. The son of a German immigrant who had made a fortune in timber and iron-ore holdings in the Midwest and who died when Bill was only eight, Boeing left Yale University in 1903, at the age of 22, and moved to the Pacific Northwest. There he followed in his father's footsteps and made a small fortune in timberlands.

A tall, mustachioed man whose thin-rimmed glasses gave him a professorial look, he had a quiet manner that belied his thirst for adventure and his pursuit of expensive hobbies. His fondness for sailing led him to buy a small Seattle boatyard so that he could build a yacht of his own design. But he became even more intrigued with planes. After going aloft in a floatplane over Seattle's Lake Washington in 1914 he decided to try making a similar craft himself, and put the boatyard to work on the project. Meanwhile he went to Los Angeles to take flying lessons at the school run by the great pioneer airman Glenn Martin. After finishing the course he bought a Martin seaplane, just to compare it with the one he was building.

Boeing's own plane proved so well designed that he took $100,000 of his funds and set up an aircraft-manufacturing company at the boatyard. In 1917, with the United States at war in Europe, the Boeing Airplane Company landed a contract to build seaplanes for the Navy; needing good help, he hired two recent University of Washington graduates, Claire L. Egtvedt and Philip G. Johnson. Egtvedt was a gifted engineer and designer, while Johnson, though trained as an engineer, turned out to be a born salesman and a talented organizer. Before long, Boeing was attending mainly to finances, and the two young men were running the company.

With the end of the War, the company's military sales dried up. For a while Boeing kept the plant going by making furniture, but a civilian use for his aircraft sooned turned up. Steamships bound from Seattle to the Orient stopped at Victoria, at the southern tip of Canada's Vancouver Island, 74 miles across Puget Sound, before heading out to sea. Edward Hubbard, a test-pilot friend of Boeing's, had the idea that late mail could be flown to Victoria to be put on board ship; the plane could return to Seattle carrying mail just brought in by incoming vessels. And Bill Boeing had developed a new craft, the B-1 flying boat, that would be well suited to the task.

The two men formed a partnership and won permission from Canadian and United States authorities to start such a service. They made their first trip on March 3, 1919. Thereafter, Hubbard generally flew alone; sometimes Boeing would substitute, just to keep his hand in. The flights shuttled back and forth through the early and middle 1920s, gaining exposure for Boeing's planes and experience for both partners in operating an airline, albeit a small one.

Meanwhile, the Army and Navy began expanding their air arms, and Boeing was again preoccupied with plane making at the time that the first domestic mail contracts were put up for bids. In the fall of 1926, however, Eddie Hubbard heard some news that led him to come up with another brainstorm. The Post Office, having awarded most of the feeder contracts during the previous year, had disclosed that it was ready to call for bids on the United States transcontinental trunk route.

The lucrative route was to be divided into two legs—one from New York to Chicago and the other from Chicago to San Francisco—and separate bids were solicited for each leg. Hubbard roared into Egtvedt's office—Johnson was in Washington trying to sell planes to the Navy—and insisted that Boeing bid on the Chicago-San Francisco leg. "This is the opportunity of a century, Claire," he cried. Egtvedt, caught by surprise, remarked that it was a huge undertaking filled with new challenges, such as flying during the winter and at night. But Hubbard

Young Bill Boeing (right) brings a sack of letters ashore in Seattle, Washington, after the first Canada-to-United States mail flight in 1919. The seaplane he and pilot Eddie Hubbard (left) flew from Victoria, British Columbia, was a modified version of the Model C trainers Boeing built for the United States Navy during World War I.

continued to press his case. Egtvedt had recently designed a new mail-plane, the Boeing Model 40, for the Post Office. The craft had not gone into production because the government had chosen instead the rival Douglas M-3, which was similar to the M-2 now being used by Pop Hanshue's Western Air Express. The two men agreed that the new Boeing craft, if modified and given a better engine, might be able to fly the difficult route. Flushed with excitement, they went to Bill Boeing's downtown office and laid out their proposition.

Boeing listened carefully, but he seemed wary. "This is something foreign to our experience," he finally said. "It would be a mighty large venture. Mighty risky." Hubbard and Egtvedt left, suspecting that nothing would come of the visit. But the following morning when Egtvedt arrived at his office, he was told that Boeing had been trying for an hour to reach him. The boss was obviously excited when the two men reappeared in his office. Their proposal had kept him up all night, he said. And the more he thought about it the more promising it seemed. They talked some more about the bid, and then Boeing announced: "These figures look all right to me. Let's send them in."

In vying for the long route Boeing faced a formidable competitor: Pop Hanshue was also seeking the route, and he had bid what he considered an extremely low figure on behalf of his Western Air Express: $2.24 per pound of mail for the first 1,000 miles and 24 cents for each additional 100 miles. But when the bids were opened in Washington, a dismayed Hanshue learned that he had been substantially underbid by Boeing, who had offered to fly the mail for only $1.50 a pound for the first 1,000 miles and just 15 cents for each additional 100 miles. In short, Boeing was offering to carry mail more than halfway across the continent for no more than the Post Office was then paying to send it from New York to Boston. Hanshue, like nearly everyone else in the airline industry, was certain that Boeing would go broke, but he surprised them all. The new service, organized as Boeing Air Transport, got under way on July 1, 1927; it took on seasoned former Post Office pilots and made money right from the beginning.

The key to Boeing's success, as Hubbard and Egtvedt had predicted, was the Model 40A airplane, redesigned to carry two passengers in an enclosed cabin and equipped with a powerful new air-cooled Pratt & Whitney engine that was 222 pounds lighter than the craft's original power plant. Frederick Rentschler, the creative and foresighted Pratt & Whitney executive who was responsible for the engine, was an old friend of Bill Boeing's, and there were similarities between them: German-American background, love of speed and fascination with aviation. But while Boeing was quiet-mannered and introverted, Rentschler was brash and gregarious. Born into a Midwestern family, he had done a stint in his father's foundry, and during World War I he worked at the Wright-Martin Aircraft Company's New Jersey plant, which was making Hispano-Suiza engines for Allied warplanes. Following the Armistice in 1918, Wright-Martin was reorganized as the Wright Aeronautical Company; Rentschler, barely 30, was named president.

At the time, the American aircraft engine industry was embroiled in a design controversy. The best engines of the day were water-cooled, with in-line cylinders much like those of an automobile. But an innovator named Charles Lawrance had produced an air-cooled radial engine whose cylinders were ranged around a central hub. While not yet as powerful as water-cooled models, it seemed to offer greater potential. Engine men were divided on the subject, but the Navy believed so firmly in Lawrance's design that it stopped ordering conventional engines from Wright Aeronautical. Wright bought out the small Lawrance company to acquire its technology and was rewarded with large orders that quickly made the new radial engines widely available for both military and civilian aircraft.

One result of this move was the famous 200-horsepower J-5C Whirlwind engine, which was to power Charles Lindbergh's *Spirit of St. Louis* across the Atlantic Ocean in May of 1927. But Rentschler was not content with the Whirlwind, and he was convinced that a still-better engine could be built. Wright's board of directors put him off—the company was doing well enough with the Whirlwind, they said, so why sink money into something unproved? Rentschler then resigned, intending to set up his own company. Seeking financial support, he turned to his brother Gordon, who was executive vice president of New York's National City Bank.

Gordon Rentschler happened to have on his desk a report on a machine-tool concern that owned a subsidiary in Hartford, Connecticut. The subsidiary, Pratt & Whitney, had a sizable cash surplus but was currently idle; the company had never made airplane engines, but it had a reputation for precision work. Frederick Rentschler persuaded Pratt & Whitney to stake him in the proposed venture and brought over from Wright Aeronautical his top engineer and his best designer. They set to work in the summer of 1925; at the end of March 1926 they were ready to give their first engine a stationary test. Rentschler's wife was present and liked its rasping roar. She gave it a name: the Wasp. The Navy liked the engine, too, and for good reason—it developed 420 horsepower, more than double that of the Wright Whirlwind. And before long Pratt & Whitney was working at top speed to build 200 Wasps for the Navy's new carrier aircraft.

Bill Boeing and Claire Egtvedt were certain that the Boeing Model 40, though designed to be powered by a water-cooled engine, could easily be adapted to accommodate the new Wasp. With Rentschler's help they persuaded the Navy to defer its own order and to let Boeing have 25 of the new engines right away. The redesigned Model 40A was rushed into production with only a bare minimum of testing, and when it performed superbly on the Chicago-to-San Francisco run, Bill Boeing was one of the few people who were not surprised. The secret was in the Wasp's light weight, he said: It enabled him to carry passengers

An airline founded to outwit outlaws

In 1924, Mexico was enjoying an economic boom, thanks to the discovery of oil near the Gulf city of Tampico on its northeastern coast. But the oil bonanza was sorely taxed by the region's rural bandits who, lured by the gold dollars paid to oil-field workers, regularly waylaid and robbed the drilling company paymasters traveling by road to the isolated fields some 90 miles inland.

The situation had become desperate when an American banker in Tampico, George Rihl, hit upon an idea inspired by the appearance of some itinerant American barnstormers: Why not buy out the airmen, he reasoned, and fly the payrolls over the earthbound *bandidos'* heads? On August 20, 1924, Rihl set up the Compañía Mexicana de Aviación, with headquarters in Tampico, bought the planes and hired former United States Army aviators to fly them.

The airline delivered the payrolls safely and promptly and expanded to provide passenger and mail service to Veracruz, Tejería and Mexico City. To shore up his finances, Rihl later sold company shares to American firms, including Pan American Airways. But Mexicana remained a Mexican corporation, enabling it justly to claim the honor of being that country's first scheduled airline as well as one of the oldest commercial carriers in the Western Hemisphere.

Mexicana's fleet of four Lincoln Standard biplanes and a Fairchild FC-2W2 airliner (center) is assembled on the landing field near the city of Tampico in 1928.

A jitney ferries Mexicana passengers from the landing field at Tejería to Veracruz in 1928. The line was one of the first to offer ground transport for its passengers.

and mail across the Rocky Mountains instead of radiators and water.

Boeing made Phil Johnson president of his now thriving airline and installed Eddie Hubbard as vice president in charge of operations. Claire Egtvedt became general manager of the aircraft-manufacturing company. With such capable executives in control it was possible now to consider further moves, and they were not long in coming.

Vern Gorst, seeking to upgrade his Pacific Air Transport, came to Seattle in late 1927 to see about buying some Boeing 40As for his fleet. The selling price of $25,000 each was far out of reach for the perpetually hard-pressed Gorst, and when Pat Patterson advised that it would be to his advantage to sell out to Boeing, Gorst agreed—provided Boeing would keep Pacific Air's employees on the payroll and buy up all the outstanding shares that Gorst had distributed so lavishly to his pilots and suppliers.

The deal was struck, and thus began a period of corporate expansion that would soon make Boeing a giant of the air transport industry. In the fall of 1928 the company formed Boeing Airplane and Transport Corporation as a holding company for its Seattle-based manufacturing and airline operations and for Pacific Air, which continued to do business under its own name. Early the next year Bill Boeing and the engine-builder Fred Rentschler—by then the head of Pratt & Whitney—agreed to combine their two concerns into still another holding company, United Aircraft and Transport Corporation. United soon added to its stable a number of other aviation enterprises, among them Stout Air Services and several manufacturing concerns.

Along with the other air carriers that had sprung up in the middle 1920s, the United lines were now ready to capitalize on a growing public interest in air travel. This interest had been strongly spurred by Charles Lindbergh's epic solo flight across the North Atlantic in May of 1927, a feat of personal daring that captured the popular imagination and did more than perhaps any other event of the decade to demonstrate the airplane's vast potential.

But public interest alone was not quite enough to spark a significant growth in commercial aviation. Before large numbers of passengers would take to the air, some of the hazards of flying would have to be overcome. Fortunately for the United States airline industry—and for the traveling public as well—help was at hand from the wealthy Guggenheim family of New York.

Harry Guggenheim, the scion of that copper-rich clan, had been a Navy flier in World War I and had subsequently convinced his father, Daniel Guggenheim, of aviation's potential and of its need for technical development. So the Guggenheims in the late 1920s set up schools of aeronautical engineering at a number of universities, sponsored the painting of town names on rooftops to aid in navigation and helped to develop instruments that would make it possible for pilots to fly safely at night and in foggy weather.

In 1928 the Guggenheims went beyond such technical matters and

A promotional postcard displays one of the three Fokker Trimotors used to launch a Western Air Express experimental passenger service in 1928. Underwritten by the Daniel Guggenheim Fund to help promote air travel, the service introduced lunches and radio programs in flight, and limousine service on the ground.

sought to show that a well-equipped passenger airline could turn a profit even without a mail subsidy from the government. To carry out the test they offered to stake Pop Hanshue's Western Air Express to five brand-new transport planes to fly a passengers-only Model Air Line from Los Angeles to San Francisco. Hanshue chose 12-passenger Fokker Trimotors powered by Wasp engines. Public response was cordial: Some 5,000 persons flew the line the first year, and the Trimotors chalked up a 99 per cent on-time record and suffered no fatal accidents.

Despite its apparent success, the line did not make money, though Hanshue was able to cover his losses with mail-contract revenue from other routes. And the popularity of the model line encouraged airline men to look ahead to a day when their primary business might be the transportation of passengers rather than mail.

Indeed, passenger traffic on United States airlines leaped in 1929 from the previous year's 60,000 persons to more than 160,000, surpassing for the first time the well-established German airlines and nearly topping the totals of all other European nations combined. Investors, once reluctant to put their money behind airline ventures, changed their tune and made aviation stocks a darling of Wall Street.

There was ample reason for their enthusiasm, though not all of them were as fortunate as some insiders who had gotten in on the ground floor. At United Aircraft and Transport, for example, one Pratt & Whitney executive saw his $40 cash investment in 1926 blossom until three years later it was worth more than three million dollars. A $253 investment by United's president, Fred Rentschler, had increased by the spring of 1929 to an astounding $35.6 million. So frenzied did the trading in aviation stocks become that there was even a small boom in securities of the Seaboard Air Line—a corporation that was in fact a somewhat anemic East Coast railroad.

If some investors were confused by the growing complexity of the airline industry, such was not the case among more sophisticated Wall Streeters. Indeed, while Pop Hanshue and others had been laying out commercial air lanes in the Western states, a number of Eastern entrepreneurs had been doing the same thing in their part of the country. And some of them had not been content with remaining east of the Mississippi River.

Foremost among these Eastern airline promoters was Clement M. Keys, a studious Canadian-born financial wizard who had started his business career by working as a reporter on the *Wall Street Journal*. Keys soon formed his own investment business, and at the end of the First World War he bought control of the Curtiss Aeroplane and Motor Company, which he used as a springboard for entry into other aviation ventures. In 1925 he formed a holding company, North American Aviation Incorporated, and he made his first big expansion move in the same year, when he organized an airline, National Air Transport. The line quickly won the valuable airmail route between Chicago and Dallas, flying by way of Kansas City and carrying an occasional passenger.

In April 1927, National was awarded the coveted eastern leg of the transcontinental mail route; it began flying this New York-Chicago run not long after Boeing Air Transport started its service between Chicago and San Francisco. But while Boeing hauled passengers right from the start, National limited itself to the mail; Keys did not want to risk passenger flights across the treacherous Allegheny Mountains. Then in 1928 he solved this problem by establishing a combination air-rail system for coast-to-coast travelers.

Keys called his new company, organized in cooperation with the Pennsylvania and Santa Fe Railroads, Transcontinental Air Transport, or TAT—pilots referred to it as "take a train." To give it additional prestige he signed up Charles Lindbergh as technical consultant, a move that permitted him to advertise TAT as "the Lindbergh line." But while Lindbergh had crossed the Atlantic in a single nonstop flight, passengers on TAT made the two-day journey across the continent in grueling stages, riding Pullman sleepers by night and flying in noisy Ford Tri-motors by day (pages 72-79).

Other companies tried similar experiments, but none lasted; TAT itself lost $2.7 million in a year and a half. But its parent, North American Aviation, remained strong, buoyed by its manufacturing interests, by an expanding National Air Transport operation, and by the purchase in mid-1929 of a lucrative airmail route from New York to Miami. Called Pitcairn Aviation after its founder, the aircraft manufacturer Harold Pitcairn, the New York-to-Miami line was soon given the new name of Eastern Air Transport.

As the 1920s came to a close another emerging giant of the airline industry was the Aviation Corporation, called AVCO for short, a holding company that was launched in early 1929 by a powerful group of financiers that included W. Averill Harriman and Robert Lehman. AVCO was a latecomer to the aviation world, but it quickly made up for lost time by gobbling up a wide variety of aeronautical enterprises. First to be absorbed by AVCO was Embry-Riddle, a modest company that flew between Cincinnati and Chicago. AVCO then acquired Colonial Airways Corporation, which controlled the valuable New York-Boston airmail contract and several other northeastern routes. Next, the company bought out a promising Texas-based line called Southern Air Transport; this was followed by the purchase of Universal Aviation Corporation, which was itself a holding company that operated a number of airlines in the Midwest and Southwest, among them Robertson, Central and Continental.

AVCO had meanwhile been buying up airports, engine plants and instrument manufacturers, bringing its total holdings to more than 80 separate operations. So widespread were the company's activities, in fact, that it was said that no AVCO executive was able to name all of the holding company's affiliates. Then in late 1929 the directors brought some order to their far-flung structure by setting up still another holding

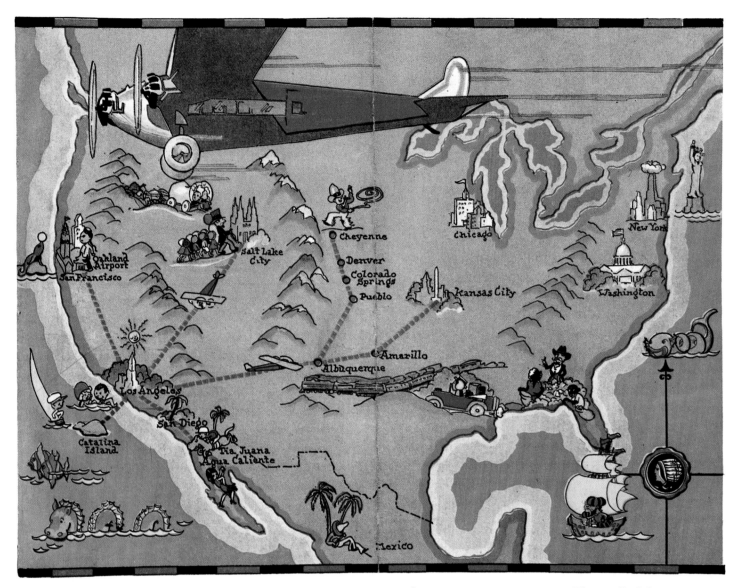

This 1929 Western Air Express route map reflects the company's phenomenal growth. Western had started in 1926 flying mail between Salt Lake City and Los Angeles. After three years its 4,700-mile system and its 39-plane fleet made it the nation's largest domestic airline.

company to run the air-transport operations. They called the new organization American Airways.

A number of independent carriers continued to ply the nation's air lanes. But with the formation of American Airways and the continued growth of United Aircraft, Eastern Air Transport and the well-financed Transcontinental Air Transport—which in late 1929 bought out a thriving California-based company called Maddux Air Lines—most of the major airlines in the United States had been brought under the control of large aviation combines. The heads of these expanding companies were now ready to wage rough-and-tumble corporate battle for dominance of the domestic airways. But neither they nor their unaffiliated competitors had reckoned on the spirited intervention in their affairs of an Ohio lawyer and politician named Walter Folger Brown. Although he had no previous experience in aviation, Brown would soon step in to become the dominant figure in shaping the course of American commercial air transport.

Crossing the continent on wings and rails

In 1929, the quickest way for a traveler to get across the United States was by rail: 72 hours from New York to Los Angeles on the fastest train. Although a plane could make the trip in less time, no airline was yet willing to attempt it on a regular basis because of the hazards of night flying. Then airline promoter Clement M. Keys hit on a compromise scheme: With the cooperation of the Pennsylvania and Santa Fe Railroads he organized a new system that spanned the continent by a combination of rail and air.

Transcontinental Air Transport, or TAT, as the carrier was called, started service in July 1929, moving passengers overnight by train from New York to Columbus, Ohio, and from there by alternate plane-Pullman stages to Los Angeles, making the trip in 48 hours. TAT operated eastbound as well as westbound.

From the start, the service was for the luxury trade. Passengers on the TAT Ford Tri-motors enjoyed films and hot meals. But TAT never thrived. With the fare set at a then-princely $350, the 10-seat planes were rarely more than half-filled, and TAT lost money steadily. The train-plane service was shut down after 16 months, but in 1930 TAT merged with another airline to form one of the first all-air transcontinental carriers, TWA.

A TAT passenger leaves New York on a train-plane trip to the West Coast.

A Ford Tri-motor of the type pictured in TAT ads (inset) is

displayed in New York's Pennsylvania Station to promote the new service.

A crowd at TAT's terminus near Columbus, Ohio, waits for the takeoff of the inaugural westbound flight on July 8, 1929.

TAT passengers survey the landscape from the cabin of a Ford Tri-motor. Each of the 10 cane-backed seats had a window, and passengers were given "flight logs" to chart their progress across the country.

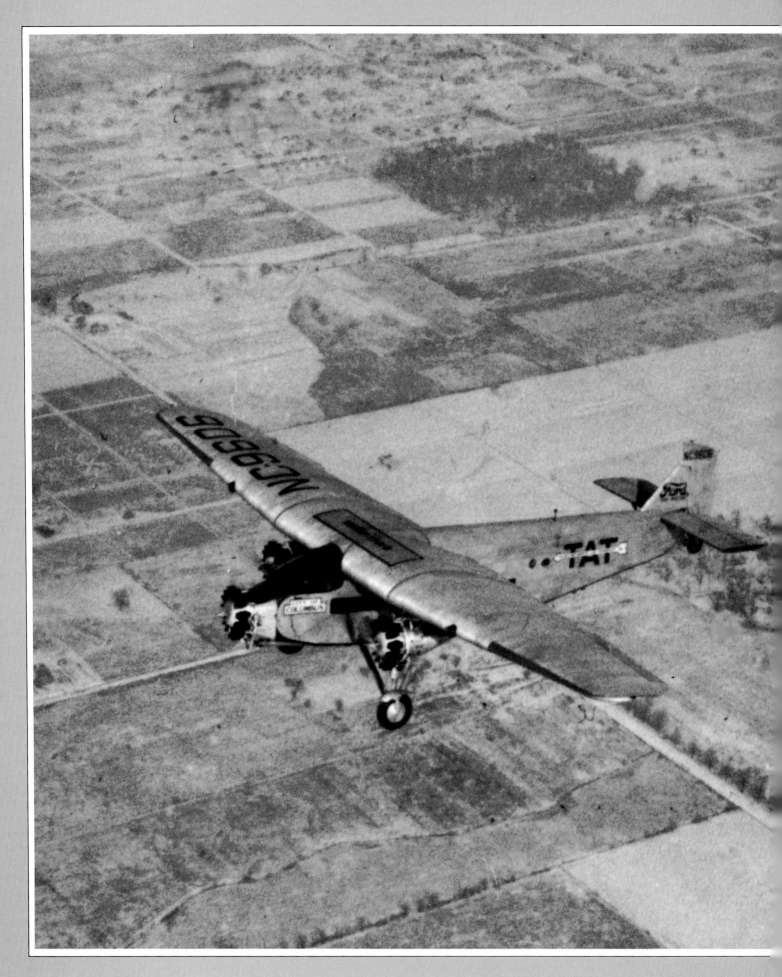

Passengers leave a TAT Aerocar to board
a plane. Used to transport passengers
between train stations and airports, the
Ford-built Aerocar was a two-wheeled steel
trailer towed by an automobile. The car's
interior was upholstered in leather.

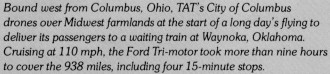

Bound west from Columbus, Ohio, TAT's City of Columbus
drones over Midwest farmlands at the start of a long day's flying to
deliver its passengers to a waiting train at Waynoka, Oklahoma.
Cruising at 110 mph, the Ford Tri-motor took more than nine hours
to cover the 938 miles, including four 15-minute stops.

After piloting TAT's first flight into Los Angeles, Charles Lindbergh (third from right) joins the passengers, including Amelia Earhart (with flowers).

EDDIE RICKENBACKER—EASTERN

JACK FRYE—TWA

W. A. "PAT" PATTERSON—UNITED

C. R. SMITH—AMERICAN

3
The forging of the Big Four

Fresh from President Herbert Hoover's inaugural ceremonies in March of 1929, incoming Postmaster General Walter Folger Brown sat at his imposing mahogany desk and perused the leatherbound portfolio describing his new duties. One phrase especially caught his eye: It would be his role "to encourage commercial aviation"—which, of course, included passenger airlines—and to "contract for the Air Mail service." The challenge intrigued him, and when he went into action he would revolutionize the American airline industry.

There was nothing new about the responsibilities of Brown's position. Although the Post Office Department was not the sole federal agency concerned with aeronautics, only the Postmaster General was charged with awarding lucrative government contracts that could keep a commercial air carrier in business. Indeed, Brown's predecessors had been tinkering with the airmail for more than a decade. But Brown was a public servant who liked to do things his own way. A stickler for protocol, he insisted on wearing a top hat while on official business and ordered his department to provide a limousine with a ceiling high enough so that he could ride fully hatted to his appointments. Brown had been schooled in the rough Ohio politics of Republican leader Mark Hanna and he was an operator of rare intelligence and skill. He knew little about the airline business when he took office, but he set about educating himself; before long he had come to know more about the industry than nearly anyone in it. And the more he learned, the more he felt that firm action was needed.

For one thing, the way the airlines were paid to carry the mail was becoming absurd. In 1928 airmail postage rates had been cut in order to encourage public usage, but the airlines were still being paid by weight—an arrangement that enabled many contractors to receive subsidies that exceeded the postage on the letters they carried. Some of them saw in this an easy way to fatten their income, and began swelling their revenues by mailing letters to themselves. One line sent out hundreds of Christmas cards, each costing approximately nine cents including postage, but bringing in 18 cents in revenue. It was, observed a recipient of one of the cards, "a nice combination of good will to man and business sense."

The new Postmaster General was incensed by such tactics. And his strong sense of order was offended by a growing turbulence in the

In the 1930s these men, the presidents of the Big Four, helped to establish their airlines as America's principal carriers. Despite the diversity of their backgrounds— Rickenbacker was a legendary war ace, Patterson a successful banker—each left his company with the indelible mark of his strong and capable personality.

airline business. Spurred by investor interest in aviation stocks and by the availability of mail-contract revenues, new lines were cropping up nearly everywhere providing the nation with an extensive but largely uncoordinated system of air transport. And the more centralized holding companies sometimes seemed to be expending almost as much of their energy in fighting among themselves as they did in running efficient airline operations.

An especially bitter clash came to a climax in early 1930 and pitted Fred Rentschler and his United Aircraft against Clement Keys and his North American Aviation. At issue was a North American subsidiary company, National Air Transport, which held the Chicago-New York mail contract. United could bring mail and passengers from San Francisco to Chicago on its Boeing Air Transport planes but could not carry them on to New York. Seeking to extend his service into New York, Rentschler proposed to merge the two lines into a single transcontinental system. Keys refused even to consider such a move; Rentschler thereupon set out to acquire National Air Transport with tactics that were in the best tradition of the old railroad robber barons.

Rentschler's plan was to challenge Keys at the annual NAT stockholders' meeting, which was scheduled for April 10. Working quietly, he bought up nearly a third of the line's outstanding shares from a group of Chicago investors. When word of the purchase appeared in the press, he explained grandly: "From an economic point of view, the air between the coasts is not big enough to be divided." He then called upon other NAT stockholders to authorize him to vote their shares by proxy at the annual meeting.

Keys, equally adept at corporate warfare, fought back. Three days before the meeting, he persuaded his directors to issue 300,000 shares of additional NAT stock—thus erasing Rentschler's numerical advantage—and exchange them for shares in North American Aviation, the holding company that was firmly in the hands of Keys and his associates. Outmaneuvered at the stockholders' meeting, Rentschler attacked Keys in court and won an injunction against the new stock issue. Continuing his attack, he bought up still more NAT shares; by April 17, he had cornered 57 per cent of the line's stock. For Clement Keys, the battle was over. On April 23 the victorious Frederick Rentschler was elected chairman and president of National Air Transport, which soon became an operating arm of the wide-ranging United Aircraft. (Only two months afterward, United Aircraft added Varney Air Lines to its roster of acquisitions.)

The nation now had its first truly transcontinental airline. But to Postmaster General Walter Brown's mind, this was merely the beginning. He was convinced that an efficient commercial air-transport system demanded several well-financed and competitive transcontinental lines plus a network of well-located feeder lines—all of them using bigger and better planes that could carry greater numbers of passengers. For if passenger traffic expanded, the mail subsidy might in due course be decreased or even eliminated altogether. Furthermore, such a vigorous air-transport industry could help strengthen national defense by encouraging manufacturers to build faster and safer aircraft that would also be suitable for military purposes.

Armed with these convictions, Brown proceeded in early 1930 to lobby in Congress for changes in the way the government chose and paid the airlines that carried the mail. The resulting McNary-Watres Act, drafted by Brown and passed by Congress on April 29, 1930, provided that airlines would be paid not by pounds of mail per mile, but by the amount of space available for mail. Large planes would thus earn more than small ones, even if they happened to carry no mail at all on a particular trip. The new regulations also provided bonuses for multi-engined craft equipped with better navigational devices. In one stroke, Brown hoped not only to eliminate the sneaky revenue-gouging practices of some of the marginal airlines but to promote the use of capacious craft that could carry large numbers of fare-paying passengers.

The key sections of the Watres Act, as it came to be called, also empowered the Postmaster General to bypass low bids for a competitive airmail contract and award the route instead to the "lowest responsible bidder." All but the most experienced air carriers were thus ruled out of the airmail business, for the Act defined a responsible bidder as one that had flown daily scheduled service over a 250-mile route for a period of at least six months—and Brown stiffened this definition by requiring that such service must have been offered both day and night. In addition, the Postmaster General won the right to extend or consolidate existing routes "when in his judgment the public interest will be promoted thereby."

The members of Congress may not have realized it, but they had given Brown virtual dictatorial powers over the airlines. And he did not hesitate to exercise his new authority.

Barely two weeks after passage of the Watres Act, Brown summoned the heads of the country's major airlines to his office in Washington. There he told them of his bold plan to reshape their industry. United Aircraft's recently established service from New York to San Francisco was an admirable achievement, he said. But United could not be permitted to have a coast-to-coast monopoly. Instead, there must be competition in the form of two more transcontinental lines, one of them flying a central route from New York to Los Angeles via such points as Pittsburgh and St. Louis, the other following a southern course from New York and Washington to Atlanta and on to Los Angeles by way of Dallas and Oklahoma City. Brown further decreed that each of the new routes had to be serviced by a single company, not by an amalgam of airlines with connecting flights. The Postmaster General suggested that the assembled executives meet among themselves to work out the details and report back to him.

The airline men had scant enthusiasm for Brown's proposals, but

Swarming bombers mark the 1930 opening of an airport built at Burbank, California, by the company that later became United Air Lines.

they had little choice in the matter. Brown, after all, would award the lucrative airmail contracts, and he thus held the airlines firmly by their purse strings. Still, the executives were too competitive and distrustful of one another to sit down and reshape their industry to the satisfaction of the Postmaster General. It was not long before they turned to Brown and asked him to "act as umpire in settling and working out such voluntary rearrangements as might be necessary" to lay out the transcontinental lines that he had called for.

Brown wasted no time. Over the next several weeks he met in his office with industry leaders to redraw the airline map of the United States. To fly the central route across the country, he chose Transcontinental Air Transport, the coast-to-coast train-plane combination. But Transcontinental, while it was well financed, had never flown at night. To meet his own definition of a responsible bidder for a coast-to-coast mail contract, Brown determined that Transcontinental would have to consolidate with most of Western Air Express, whose long night-flying experience would then qualify the combined company.

Pop Hanshue, Western's peppery and independent founder, had already spurned one merger bid from Transcontinental, and was no more enthusiastic about the idea now. Asked at one point during the discussions what he thought about the proceedings, he snapped: "I think you're all crazy as hell!" But he gave in to Brown's demands—to do otherwise might well have cost him all of Western's mail contracts. The new line was called Transcontinental and Western Air, or TWA; many years later, when TWA began to fly internationally, it preserved its initials in a new name, Trans World Airlines.

If Brown had run roughshod over Pop Hanshue in laying out the central route, he was no more gentle when he put together the southern transcontinental line. Delta Air Service, a former crop-dusting operation that flew passengers between Birmingham and Dallas, had hoped to be a contender for the route, but it was disqualified for lack of night-flying experience. The Postmaster General, in fact, did not even invite Delta founder Collett Everman Woolman to attend the meetings in Washington at which the new coast-to-coast lines were formed. Rebuffed by Walter Brown, Woolman bowed out of the airline picture and went back to crop dusting.

Another airline executive, Erle Halliburton, refused to retire so gracefully from the field. A rambunctious Oklahoma oil tycoon—and a cousin of the famed author-adventurer Richard Halliburton—Halliburton owned a bustling, Tulsa-based company called Southwest Air Fast Express, known for short as SAFEway. He dreamed of building his little operation into a great transcontinental system, and had tried earlier to undercut other airlines in mail-contract bids. But Brown had deemed him unreliable and had refused to listen to him.

Denied admittance to the conferences in Brown's office, Halliburton appealed, through an influential friend, all the way to the White House, and won the right to attend. It did him little good, however: Inside

Walter Folger Brown, who used his powers as Postmaster General to drastically redraw the United States airways map, was renowned for his impeccable dress as well as his political acumen. A Harvard-educated lawyer from Toledo, Ohio, Brown also loved to sail, cook and camp.

the Post Office building, he was virtually ignored and had to resort to heckling to make his points. Worse still, Brown would not even consider Halliburton's bid on the southern route or on any other mail run, on the ground that SAFEway lacked experience in night flying. Halliburton retorted that this requirement was not even contained in the Watres Act, but that it had simply been imposed by the Postmaster General. Finally, the scrappy Oklahoman threatened to take his case to the federal courts.

Brown and his coterie of favored airline operators had now had quite enough of Halliburton's obstructionist maneuvers. Having agreed that the coveted southern route would be awarded to the recently formed American Airways system, the executives moved—presumably with encouragement from Brown—to silence Halliburton's objections by buying him out. American got the route, paying Halliburton $1.4 million for his airline—which was, by his own reckoning, worth little more than half that amount.

With the settlement of the southern transcontinental issue, Walter Folger Brown had achieved his goal of providing the United States with a coherent and competitive air-transport system that was capable of solid growth in the future. But what was good for the nation was not necessarily good for all the airline companies that had been involved in Brown's machinations.

Western Air Express and the United system, the two lines that had been considered the most successful in pre-Brown days, did not benefit at all. United, the coast-to-coast trailblazer, quickly lost some 40 per cent of its revenue to its new transcontinental competitors. After the forced merger with TAT, Western had been permitted to operate separately under its own name over a few of its shorter routes, but it lost so much money that it almost went under and was rescued only when General Motors stepped in and bought a controlling interest. Pop Hanshue, meanwhile, had taken over the presidency of TWA, but he did not get along with his former adversaries and was dismissed after just eight months on the job. Even at that, United and Western had fared far better than many other companies. Strewn all about the landscape were the shattered hopes of small airline operators who were made to realize that from Walter Brown's perspective the commercial air lanes belonged to the supercompanies, no matter how successfully a smaller company might be run.

One of the companies caught by the Brown steam roller was the Ludington Air Lines Inc. Named after two of its principal backers, a pair of wealthy Philadelphia brothers named Charles and Nicholas Ludington, this ambitious little airline linked New York and Washington with passengers-only flights leaving every hour on the hour. Rigorous cost cutting was Ludington's byword. Its aircraft, inexpensive Stinson Tri-Motors, taxied on just one engine instead of all three; after using expensive high-test fuel while taking off, they cruised on ordinary automobile fuel, which was cheaper.

Such economies made Ludington the first airline in history to turn a profit without any form of government assistance. The Ludingtons were certain to have a bonanza on their hands if only they could acquire the New York-Washington mail contract. But Postmaster General Brown, determined to encourage the continued growth of large and well-established operations, rejected the Ludingtons' low bid in the summer of 1931 and gave the contract to Eastern Air Transport—whose bid was more than three times that of the Ludington Line. Eastern began putting newer and larger planes on the New York-Washington run; Ludington, its passengers lured away by such well-heeled competition, held on for more than a year. But the line finally bowed to the inevitable and sold out to Eastern in early 1933.

By then, the nation's commercial aviation system seemed to be running smoothly and in accordance with Walter Brown's grand design. Transcontinental flying was competitive. Airlines everywhere were seeking larger and faster planes. Passenger traffic was increasing steadily and the nation's 27,000 miles of air lanes were dominated by four major carriers: American, TWA, Eastern, and United Air Lines, organized in 1931 as the management company for United Aircraft's four transport companies, which continued to operate under their own names. And if mail contracts were not necessarily going to the lowest bidder, the taxpayer's burden was down: In 1929 the Post Office had paid an average of $1.10 per mile to fly the mail; by 1933 the figure was down to 54 cents. But the nation's airline operators were about to run into some severe political turbulence.

When Ludington lost out to Eastern for the New York-Washington airmail run, a Ludington employee mentioned the line's misfortune to a friend, a young newspaper reporter named Fulton Lewis Jr. Lewis was astounded to learn that Eastern's higher bid had beat out Ludington's lower figure, and soon got approval from his publisher, William Randolph Hearst, to conduct a thorough investigation of Postmaster General Brown's handling of airmail contracts.

Lewis finished his work in January of 1932. Certain that he had an explosive story on his hands, Lewis sent it to Hearst for approval. But the story never appeared in print, possibly because of a top Hearst editor's close friendship with the Postmaster General.

Then in March of 1933 the Hoover administration—including Walter Folger Brown—was swept out of office. The new President, Democrat Franklin D. Roosevelt, voiced the country's indignation at big-business interests that he blamed for having brought on the worst economic depression in the nation's history. That autumn, as part of a Congressional investigation into federal subsidies for transoceanic surface mail carriers, an aggressive Senator from Alabama, Hugo Black, began looking into the awarding of airmail contracts as well. Hearing of the unpublished Fulton Lewis investigation, Black prevailed upon Hearst to let him use the Lewis material in his own inquiry; not long

Cruising over a glittering grid of city lights, a Maddux Air Lines Ford Tri-motor is caught by the beam of a searchlight in this 1929 poster advertising night flying— an adventure then still new to the public.

In the mid-1930s, passengers await a night flight on an American Airlines Condor Sleeper, the first plane with convertible berths for sleeping. By that time, improved navigational aids had made night flying commonplace, and planes like the Condor allowed passengers to snooze comfortably.

afterward, he arranged for government agents to seize pertinent files from airlines throughout the country.

In the hearings that followed, the meetings at which Brown and his select group of airline executives had carved up the nation's sky lanes were characterized by critics as "spoils conferences," a sinister but perhaps not totally inaccurate assessment. And much was made of the fact that all but three of the 27 contracts awarded at the meetings had gone to airlines controlled by the giant holding companies. Black also blasted the leaders of the major airlines for their stock-market profits during the late 1920s and for their participation in what he described as illegal meetings in ex-Postmaster General Brown's office. Indeed, one of the airline executives recalled that he had once expressed to an attorney some doubts about the propriety of the proceedings. The attorney had replied: "If we were holding this meeting across the street in the Raleigh Hotel, it would be an improper meeting, but because we are holding it at the invitation of a member of the Cabinet, and in the office of the Post Office Department, it is perfectly all right."

The star witness at the hearings was Walter Brown himself, who steadfastly defended his role and insisted that he had acted in the public interest. "There was no sense," he explained, "in taking this government's money and dishing it out, giving it out as a handout to every little fellow that was flying around the map and was not going to do anything or could not do anything to develop aviation in the broad sense." In the light of this philosophy, even the rejection of the Ludington Line's rock-bottom bid for carrying the mail between Washington and New York seemed perfectly logical. As a small airline with minimal overhead Ludington could well afford to underbid Eastern, which had far more planes and flew many long and difficult routes. But Brown believed that over the long run the national interest would be better served by supporting ambitious lines such as Eastern—even at higher initial cost—than by awarding airmail contracts to smaller lines that chose to ply only the easiest and most lucrative routes.

Brown's right to make such choices would later be affirmed by the United States Court of Claims, and the route structure that he forged as Postmaster General would remain the backbone of American commercial aviation for decades to come. But Senator Black was not swayed by Brown's arguments. Instead, he remained convinced that Brown had encouraged collusion among the airlines and had broken the law by avoiding strict competitive bidding. And in late January, 1934, while his hearings were still in progress, Black urged President Roosevelt to cancel all the private carriers' airmail contracts—which Black held to be fraudulent. Roosevelt agreed, and after canceling the contracts he ordered the Army Air Corps to fly the mail.

It was a disastrous decision. Flying in open-cockpit planes, lacking the kind of navigational aids that had become standard among the airlines, poorly trained Army pilots groped their way over unfamiliar routes, fighting the worst winter weather in years. By the end of the first week five pilots were dead and six critically injured, and there was an immediate public outcry.

After the third week, Roosevelt realized that he had committed a major blunder, and he made the inevitable concession: New bids would be called for and the airlines would return to flying the mail. Pending new arrangements, the Army continued its airmail service until early May—flying only in the daytime.

Although the commercial airlines had won the right to fly the mail once more, they had not emerged unscathed from the so-called airmail emergency. Deprived of their accustomed postal revenues, almost all of them had severely curtailed their services. Pop Hanshue, who had returned to Western after his bitter tour of duty with TWA, had observed: "We're not cutting to the bone—we're cutting into the bone." All the lines had suffered financially. United Air Lines alone had lost more than $850,000 during the first quarter of 1934. And everyone in the industry knew that yet more government-imposed changes would have to be made before business could improve.

Indeed, Senator Black's hearings had led to legislation that would

In this 1934 cartoon from Aero Digest the skeletons of 12 Army pilots form an accusing parade behind Postmaster General James Farley and President Franklin D. Roosevelt. Victims of inexperience and cold weather, the 12 died during the first five weeks after Farley transferred to the Army Air Corps the job of flying airmail.

break up the giant holding companies by prohibiting any connection between an airline and a company that made aircraft or aircraft parts. And the new Postmaster General, James A. Farley, had decreed that none of the airlines involved in the 1930 "spoils conferences" could submit new bids for airmail contracts. But the four biggest and most experienced companies could hardly be ignored, and Farley was evidently willing to accept some superficial changes in name. Thus American Airways, with a perfectly straight corporate face, became American Airlines; Eastern Air Transport turned into Eastern Air Lines, and TWA got away with simply adding Inc. to its name. United, because it had not been legally present at the meetings—at that stage it had consisted of component lines still operating under their own names—continued as United Air Lines.

The sham name changes were harmless enough. A more vindictive feature of the so-called purge of the industry was the insistence that no airline could bid for a mail contract unless it rid itself of all executives who had participated in Brown's meetings. Some of the lines had changed top management in the interim, but Bill Boeing's longtime lieutenant, Phil Johnson, was still president of United Air Lines. He reluctantly pulled out and moved to Canada, where he organized and operated Trans Canada Airlines. Another casualty was that old airline warrior Pop Hanshue, who had vainly resisted Brown and the other exponents of consolidation and who now had to leave Western Air Express for the second and last time.

When Farley ripped open the sealed bids on April 20, 1934, he found that most of the routes devised by Walter Brown were to be operated by the same lines as before. The airline bosses, taking no chances of losing out at this stage, had entered rock-bottom bids in hopes that some upward adjustments would be made later—as they indeed were. Only one line suffered a significant route loss: United was outbid for its Dallas-to-Chicago run by a maverick operator named Thomas E. Braniff, an independent who would one day build his company into an international carrier. Another independent who came out ahead was the resourceful C. E. Woolman of Delta: He now had a contract to fly a mail route all the way from Charleston, South Carolina, to Dallas and Fort Worth. Woolman was to establish his line as a major carrier in the southeastern United States; much later, he would launch service across the continent from Atlanta to the Pacific Coast.

But such growth would come long and hard, and the years after 1934 turned out to be tough ones for all the airlines, both large and small; not until the beginning of the 1940s would any of them start to show an appreciable profit.

In these rigorous times America's domestic air-transport industry continued to be dominated by its so-called Big Four—TWA, United, Eastern and American. And each of these airlines was in turn dominated by a strong-willed chief executive who would leave his enduring stamp on his company. At three of the airlines, the top leader was to stay in office

Traveling ads with sticking power

The opening of United States airmail routes to private operators in 1925 triggered an explosion of commercial aviation. Some 130 new airlines sprang up within a year, increasing the number of companies to a chaotic 420. Scrambling to gain recognition, many airlines borrowed a practice from steamship companies, flooding their customers with free, eye-catching baggage stickers.

A suitcase plastered with stickers was a distinctive status symbol, identifying its owner as a member of that small elite who often traveled by air. Capitalizing on this advertising potential, many airlines detailed their routes and pictured their planes on their stickers, revising designs as the lines grew. The resulting profusion of colorful stickers serves as a remarkably informative index of airline history.

These 14 baggage stickers are a small selection from the hundreds that were issued in the 1920s and 1930s. The airlines represented here either were forced out of business or were absorbed by larger companies; by the late 1930s, all of these stickers were obsolete.

92

CARRIED BY AIR
UTAH
NPA
IDAHO
MONTANA
NATIONAL PARKS
AIRWAYS, INC.

SPEED-COURTESY-SAFETY
MARTZ
AIRLINES
WILKES BARRE, PA.

CENTURY
AIR LINES
INC.

VARNEY
VARNEY
SPEED LANES
WEST WIND
SPEED LINES

The
FLYING YANKEE
of the AIR

BOSTON-MAINE
AIRWAYS, INC.

THE
LUDINGTON LINE

every hour
on the hour

NEW YORK
PHILADELPHIA
BALTIMORE
WASHINGTON

WYOMING AIR
SERVICE, INC.

INTERSTATE
U-S
AIR MAIL
PASSENGER
CHICAGO-ATLANTA
AIRLINES
INC.

for as much as a quarter of a century. Only Jack Frye, the head of TWA, would have a somewhat briefer tenure.

Texas-born William John Frye had been a Hollywood stunt flier and flight instructor in the 1920s when he and two friends set up Standard Air Lines to ferry movie stars to vacation spots in the desert. Pop Hanshue's Western Air Express acquired Standard in 1930, and with it acquired the services of Jack Frye; the following year, after Western was merged with Transcontinental Air Transport to form TWA, Frye moved up to become the new coast-to-coast line's vice president and director of operations. Not long afterward, his search for a new type of passenger plane led to the development of the Douglas DC-1 and DC-2, the first in a long series of aircraft that would revolutionize the air-transport industry *(page 123)*. In 1934, at the age of 30, Frye was named TWA's president.

As a corporate successor of Transcontinental Air, TWA continued to call itself the Lindbergh Line, and the transatlantic hero remained available as an adviser; Frye's elevation to the top job further established the line's considerable reputation as a pilot's outfit. The burly, cheerful president himself had often flown Standard's planes across the desert, and even now felt more at ease in a cockpit than he did behind a desk. He kept up his certification as a commercial pilot and was the only major airline chief who frequently flew his line's routes. He and his pilots pioneered high-altitude passenger flight, and TWA became known as the most technically proficient airline of them all. Then, in 1938, Frye came to a critical turning point.

Always an innovator, he placed an order for five new Boeing 307 transports, the first commercial planes with pressurized passenger cabins, at a total cost of some $1.6 million. When major TWA stockholders balked at the expense and compelled him to cancel the order, Frye persuaded the quirky millionaire Howard Hughes to buy into the line. It was not long before Hughes was TWA's sole owner.

Hughes, a skilled pilot in his own right, held a number of long-distance speed records. And he was no stranger to commercial aviation, having studied the business from the ground up; among other things he had worked for two months in 1932—under an assumed name—as a copilot for American Airways.

Hughes plunged eagerly into TWA's affairs, reinstating the order for the new Boeing planes and working with Frye on plans for even more advanced aircraft. For a time TWA seemed well on its way to becoming the world's finest and best-equipped airline. But Hughes' mysterious, reclusive ways, his frequent lack of interest in making major corporate decisions and his obsession with working at a number of occupations simultaneously—movie making and airplane manufacturing among others—played havoc with the line's progress. Frye tried his best to get along with TWA's mercurial owner, but it was a losing battle; in 1947, after a series of disagreements over expansion policies, Frye was fired. No one else seemed able to last for long in the presidency, and it would

Working incognito as an American Airways copilot, 26-year-old Howard Hughes —already a famous millionaire—stows baggage for a flight in 1932. Using the alias Charles Howard, Hughes held the job two months to satisfy the same aviation itch that later induced him to buy TWA.

be many years before TWA could escape from Hughes's control and resume its orderly growth.

United Air Lines was in far steadier hands. With the forced departure of Phil Johnson in 1934, the presidency was taken over by 34-year-old Pat Patterson, the former banker who had been an adviser to Vern Gorst of Pacific Air Transport and had then helped engineer the line's purchase by Boeing Air Transport in 1928. Not long afterward, Patterson had left the Wells Fargo Bank to become Johnson's assistant; as the airline interests of Boeing's parent, United Aircraft, expanded, so did Patterson's responsibilities, and the young executive moved steadily up the corporate ranks.

One of Patterson's first major decisions would forever change the nature of in-flight passenger service, not only on United but on airlines throughout the world. In 1930 he disregarded the doubts of his front-office colleagues and accepted a proposal to hire women to serve as flight attendants—the first stewardesses *(pages 136-141)*.

Another of Patterson's decisions was even more momentous. When the airmail contracts were canceled in 1934, a number of airlines considered a complete shutdown of their operations. But they first consulted Patterson; he was operating head of the nation's strongest airline, and his reaction to the crisis would be a bellwether for the entire industry. His decision was simple and direct: No matter what the losses, United would maintain its schedules as before. Following United's lead, the other lines kept operating as best they could. If Patterson had caved in, other operations would doubtless have followed, and the whole industry might well have been swept away, leaving air transport in the United States to become the government-fostered monopoly that it already was in most of the world.

Having kept United in business during the airmail emergency, the dapper Patterson soon assumed complete control of the line. His would not be an easy task. He was once described as "looking and sounding like a small adding machine," but neither he nor United's stockholders would be pleased with the figures he came up with during his early years as president. Badly battered by continuing transcontinental competition from American and TWA and by heavy financial losses sustained during the airmail emergency, United lost more than two million dollars in 1934 and just barely broke even in 1935. The line turned a modest profit the following year, but then it slipped into a prolonged period of losses.

United's fall from its once-dominant position was due in part to the company's western origins. While United was busily building up its so-called Main Line transcontinental route—which passed through relatively few large population centers—American and TWA were building up their strength in the more populous East. Ordinarily, United might have followed a similar plan by expanding its route structure through extensions and by purchase of some of the small feeder lines that served major cities. But such moves had to be approved by the federal government—the Interstate Commerce Commission was by that time the agency in charge of commercial air transport—and government officials were not favorably disposed toward United Air Lines.

For Patterson was still smarting over cancellation of the mail contracts and the banishment of his mentor, Phil Johnson, and was doggedly pursuing a protracted lawsuit to clear Johnson's name and to recover United's lost mail revenue. (In time he would win on both counts, though United received only a token monetary award.) So it came as no surprise when, in 1936, Patterson's proposed merger with a small line serving the lucrative Washington-Detroit market was blocked by the Interstate Commerce Commission. Patterson was no more successful at getting new mail contracts from postal officials who were irritated by his legal onslaughts.

United's problems continued to mount. Its fleet of 10-seat Boeing 247s was badly outclassed by the new Douglas aircraft put into service in mid-decade by the hotly competitive TWA and American. In 1934 United had taken in three times as much money as American. By 1938, United's total revenues had slipped to less than half those of American. Also in 1938, the newly created Civil Aeronautics Authority, in one of its first major acts as civil aviation's regulatory agency, rejected United's bid to buy out Western Air Express. Not for years would United regain the government's good graces, and not until the early 1960s, with the acquisition of Capital Airlines and its lucrative routes in the eastern United States, would Patterson see his airline recapture its leadership of the industry.

There were a number of similarities between Pat Patterson and C. R. (for Cyrus Rowlett) Smith, the American Airlines executive who led his company past United and into the top position in the 1930s. The two men were the same age, both were homespun and direct, both were adept with figures—Patterson had been a bank clerk, Smith an accountant. There were differences between them, too. While Patterson was short, conservative and tactful, Smith was tall and blustery, bold and exuberantly profane.

C. R. Smith's father had walked out on the family when Smith was nine, and C. R. soon went to work as an office boy. At 16 he was a bookkeeper for a bank in Whitney, Texas; then he put himself through the University of Texas, working part-time as a federal bank examiner and operating a one-man mailing-list agency. After his graduation in 1928, he became assistant treasurer of a power company whose owner presently purchased a small airline, Texas Air Transport. Smith agreed to look after the line on a temporary basis while the owner sought a permanent manager, but he soon became fascinated with the operation and asked to stay on. He learned how to pilot a plane and even became an expert mechanic.

In early 1929, when the owner bought two other lines and combined them to form Southern Air Transport, Smith began hustling for passengers—even at this early date, when most airline chiefs were still relying heavily on mail revenue, Smith was convinced the industry's future was in carrying people. He paid Dallas hotel porters special fees for steering travelers to his planes. He catered to oil drillers and roustabouts. And he went to great lengths to see that passengers reached their destinations: When weather made it impossible to get over Texas' Guadalupe Mountains on the way to El Paso, for example, Smith had his pilots land on one side of the range, bus the customers over to the other side and then fly them on in another plane. Through it all, Smith maintained his freewheeling, informal ways: He set up his office in a hangar, typed all his own letters and liked to demonstrate his ability to kick out light bulbs that dangled on overhead cords.

When Southern was bought by the Aviation Corporation later in 1929 to form American Airways, Smith became head of the new company's southern division. Following the airmail crisis in 1934 he was elected president of the renamed American Airlines and almost immediately began to act with the boldness that would characterize his entire career. Within weeks he had placed orders for a new Douglas aircraft that would eventually be known as the DC-3. He experimented with credit plans for ticket purchases and came up with the idea of an "Admirals Club" to recognize steady customers by conferring special privileges on them. Following a series of 16 fatal airline accidents in 1936 and 1937—none of them involving American Airlines planes—Smith personally composed a series of advertisements that challenged the industry's traditional taboo about frank discussion of the public's fears about flying. The most famous was starkly headlined: "Why dodge this question: Afraid to fly?" and went on to discuss his airline's own impressive safety record.

Smith continued to use his typewriter to peck out terse memorandums to his subordinates, directing their attention to mistakes and suggesting improvements. He never seemed to stop working; indeed, during one especially busy period he put in 365 consecutive days on the job. And his drive and determination paid off handsomely for American Airlines. Between 1933 and 1937 his company's passenger volume tripled; in the next five years it increased 11-fold. By 1939, American had become the nation's foremost air carrier in terms of passenger-miles flown, and under Smith's leadership the line would hold this distinction for nearly two decades.

Occasionally, though, American was upstaged by the competition. Shortly after midnight on June 19, 1941, one of its airliners was scheduled to become the first commercial plane to touch down at the new Washington National Airport. All seemed to be going as planned until the plane that had come down from the darkness taxied to the showpiece terminal: On the craft's gleaming sides were blazoned the name of Eastern Air Lines and the company's slogan, "The Great Silver Fleet." A quick-thinking Eastern executive, hearing that the American plane would be a few minutes late, had badgered the control tower into giving precedence to an Eastern plane that was circling the field.

Edward Vernon Rickenbacker, the crusty president of Eastern Air Lines, learned of the Washington incident as he lay in a hospital recovering from near-fatal injuries received four months before in a crash of one of his own company's airliners near Atlanta, Georgia. It was not the first time that Rickenbacker's life had been in danger. Before entering the airline business he had been twice a death-defying hero, first as a daring automobile racer and then as a fighter-pilot ace and a leader of the famed 94th Aero Squadron during World War I. Ever after, he would be known as Captain Eddie.

In the early postwar years, Rickenbacker had helped to found an automobile company, but the venture failed when the firm proved unable to compete with the established automobile makers. After a stint with General Motors, Rickenbacker signed on as an executive at American Airways, where he sought vainly to arrange for the acquisition of Eastern Air Transport. Then in 1932, after getting squeezed in a corporate power struggle, Captain Eddie had a better idea: He approached his former colleagues at General Motors and convinced them that they should buy out Eastern's parent organization, North American Aviation, the complex holding company that also controlled a number of manufacturing operations. General Motors took over North American in Feb-

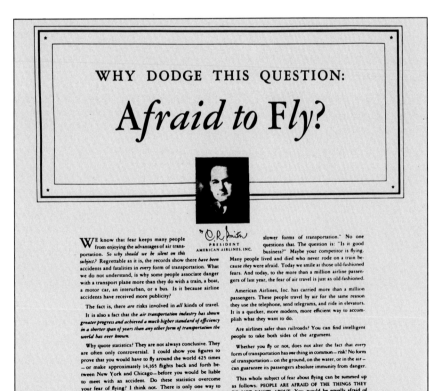

This innovative sales pitch from American Airlines President C. R. Smith boldly broke a taboo of airline advertising with its open discussion of fear of flying. Written in 1937 after an industry-wide rash of crashes, the advertisement indicated an increased interest in passenger safety.

ruary of 1933 and hired Rickenbacker as a special consultant. In the wake of the 1934 airmail crisis, Captain Eddie was named the general manager of Eastern Air Transport.

Aggressive and opinionated, Rickenbacker was a born organizer and energizer of men. He soon showed Eastern's employees that he was the boss. Among his first actions: cancellation of the free passes that had been so lavishly distributed to friendly politicians, and the summary dismissal of 19 station managers whose performance was not up to his standards. Not long afterward, he made a clean sweep of the executive suite as well. He also phased out obsolete equipment and improved operations by setting up a round-the-clock weather reporting service and laying out a new system of 23 ground radio stations.

Rickenbacker was tough and dictatorial, but his methods worked. Eastern had lost $1.5 million in 1934; in 1935 the line showed a profit of $38,000. By 1937 profits were up to nearly $200,000. But General Motors was not satisfied with its air-transport operation, and by early 1938 had quietly decided to sell Eastern Air Lines to the highest bidder and concentrate on building up North American's manufacturing operations. Rickenbacker was stunned when he heard the news, for he realized that he would be ousted by a new owner intent on running the

Passengers on a special Northwest Airlines flight in 1939 test the use of oxygen masks for sustained high-altitude travel. The rubber nose bags were reported to give wearers a "grotesque appearance, but no discomfort," and allowed pilots to climb as high as 35,000 feet.

company in his own way. Acting with characteristic dispatch, he rounded up a group of friendly Wall Streeters and with their help purchased the line for $3.5 million. Rickenbacker was installed as president, a post he would hold until the early 1950s, when he became chairman and chief executive officer.

Eastern continued to prosper and expand. Its route system, which stood at 3,358 miles in 1934, had increased to 5,381 miles by 1940, and the line that had once plied the New York-to-Miami mail route was now flying passengers, mail and cargo as far west as Chicago and San Antonio, serving a geographical area that contained 80 per cent of the United States population. In the same year, the line turned a handsome profit of more than $1.5 million.

On the night of February 26, 1941, Rickenbacker was flying in a DC-3 bound from New York to Birmingham, Alabama, where he was to address a civic group. From Birmingham he planned to fly on to Miami for a meeting with Eastern's directors, whose approval he sought for a five-million-dollar purchase of new aircraft.

Over Spartanburg, South Carolina, his plane's captain informed him that weather conditions in Atlanta, the next scheduled stopover, might pose some problems. After telling the pilot to do whatever he thought best, Captain Eddie went back to his paper work. The plane was making its final approach when Rickenbacker felt the left wing brush over some treetops. As the pilot banked violently to the right, Rickenbacker leaped from his seat and dashed for the rear of the plane, where his chance of surviving a crash might be marginally improved. Then the right wing ripped into the trees and was torn from the plane. The crippled aircraft did a nose-first somersault, landed upside down and split in two.

Trapped in the wreckage of the plane, Rickenbacker could hear the moans of the other survivors and could see that some of them were stumbling dazedly around the crumpled airliner. A steady rain was falling, and the night was cold.

"Hey, let's start a bonfire and get warm," said one passenger.

Rickenbacker, soaked in leaking fuel as well as in his own blood, summoned all his strength to shout: "No! You'll set the gasoline on fire! For God's sake, don't light a match!"

"Who is that?" came another voice from the darkness.

"Rickenbacker," rasped Captain Eddie.

A search party reached the crash site at dawn and found that nine of the 16 people on board the airliner had survived. But Rickenbacker was just barely among them. Taken to a hospital, the severely injured airline executive was given up for dead—until a Catholic priest began preparing to administer the last rites to him and Rickenbacker suddenly bellowed profanely that he was a Protestant.

Rickenbacker never completely recovered from his injuries, which included broken ribs and a crushed hip. He would walk with a limp for the rest of his life. The cause of the crash was never determined, though Rickenbacker, suspecting that a faulty altimeter might have misled the

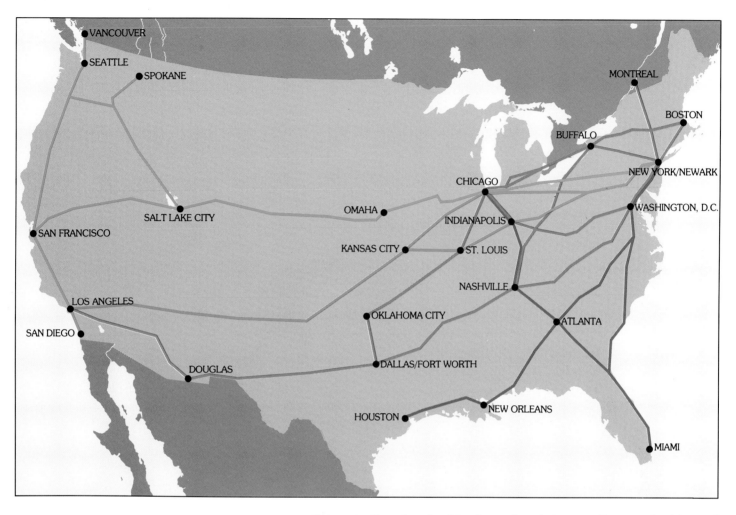

Trunk routes of America's four principal airlines in 1937 link major United States cities and some in Canada. Prior to the consolidation that created the Big Four, airlines had crisscrossed the continent with a chaotic filigree of unconnected routes.

pilot as to the plane's altitude, ordered the installation of additional precision altimeters in all of Eastern's DC-3s. The mishap did not shake his faith in the future of commercial aviation. When he was finally able to meet with his board of directors again, Rickenbacker won their approval to buy 11 more airliners for his Great Silver Fleet.

As America neared entry into World War II, its commercial airlines had come of age, built on the pattern devised by Walter Folger Brown, nurtured by the likes of Jack Frye, Pat Patterson, C. R. Smith and Eddie Rickenbacker. Indeed, by the summer of 1941 two of the Big Four, American and Eastern, were ranked among the nation's top 15 passenger carriers, along with a dozen railroads and a bus system.

But airline men alone had not made possible such tremendous strides. Plane builders, too, had done their part, frequently in close association with their colleagues and customers at the airlines. They had begun as early as the 1920s, basing their work on experiences accumulated since the days when even the most sophisticated aircraft were built of wire, wood and fabric. And then with surprising swiftness they had made new discoveries and technological advances that would usher in a revolution in aircraft design and produce the world's first truly modern airliner, the incomparable Douglas DC-3. ～

Chorus girls dance on the plywood wings of a flower-bedecked F-32 during its gala public debut at Alhambra, California, on April 17, 1930.

Hollywood hoopla for a transport that flopped

The biggest, most costly and least successful land-based airliner of its time was introduced in 1930 by Western Air Express, a forerunner of Trans World Airlines, on its San Francisco-Los Angeles run. The Fokker F-32—the number designation indicated its passenger-carrying capacity—was a trailblazer in passenger comfort and safety. It introduced reclining seats and an engine fire-extinguishing system, and it had steward call buttons, reading lights, superior instrumentation and improved visibility for the pilot. America's first four-engined aircraft, it carried two pods mounted under the wings, each holding one engine that pulled the plane and one that pushed.

For all its promise, the lumbering liner was doomed by economics. Its $110,000 price tag made it the most expensive passenger plane to buy, and it proved similarly expensive to operate. Maintenance costs skyrocketed after the government mandated frequent internal inspections of the wooden wing frames for dry rot, a procedure that required the painstaking removal of their plywood covering. The airplane could operate profitably only by carrying full loads of paying passengers, and in the depths of the Depression there simply were not enough customers.

Only two of the Fokker F-32s were actually put into service and within two years both were retired. But they provided a fleeting glimpse of what airline travel would be like only a decade in the future.

Models try out the F-32's alligator-skin seats (below), which were arranged in four spacious compartments. Each compartment held folding tables for dining (inset, far right) and could seat eight people, sleep four or be arranged (inset, near right) as a luxurious lounge graced by walnut paneling and decorator fabrics.

Once hailed as the ultimate in transport aviation, the sole surviving Fokker F-32 endured an ignominious afterlife as a Los Angeles gas station.

From sticks and string to the modern airliner

The modern airliner is descended from a long line of distinguished ancestors, eight of which are presented on these pages, in the colors of the airlines that flew them (the dates denote the year that the planes were first put into service). The first airliners, which began flying in 1919, were—not surprisingly—modified bombers. While few planes before World War I had been capable of carrying more than two persons along with the pilot, the War produced bombers with a potential passenger capacity of up to half a dozen. The passengers sat either in converted bomb bays or in open cockpits that once held machine guns. When commercial passenger aircraft began to appear in late 1919, they resembled the closed-cabin type of modified bomber.

These rudimentary airliners were of the so-called stick-and-string construction—wooden, wire-braced biplanes covered with fabric. That basic form, powered by anywhere from one to four engines, endured through most of the 1920s. Although the carrying capacity of airliners doubled in that period, their range increased only slightly and cruising speed remained about 100 miles per hour.

Metal replaced wood in the frameworks of airliners in the late 1920s. But the real breakthrough in design came in 1933, with the introduction by American builders of the light-alloy, cantilever monoplane that culminated in the DC-3. With stressed metal skin, smooth engine cowlings, wing flaps, variable pitch propellers and retractable landing gear, these planes set a pattern that would endure for 25 years. Airliners would gradually become bigger and faster, but until the arrival of the sweptwing jet, they would remain in their basic features remarkably like the DC-3.

FARMAN F.60 GOLIATH (1920)—LIGNES AÉRIENNES FARMAN
Conceived as a bomber, France's twin-engined Goliath carried a dozen passengers in its cabin, while the pilot sat in an open-air cockpit underneath the upper wing.

FOKKER F.VII (1924)—KLM ROYAL DUTCH AIRLINES
With a range of 700 miles, the single-
engined, high-winged F.VII and its trimotor
successors captured the European
market for long-distance transport planes.

FORD 4AT TRI-MOTOR (1926)—EASTERN AIR TRANSPORT
Henry Ford's all-metal Tin Goose was famed
for its toughness and its ability to land
with big loads in extremely small fields. It
was used for nearly a decade by every
major airline in the United States.

SIKORSKY S-38B(1929)—AMERICAN AIRWAYS
*The first of the great amphibious planes, the
fragile-looking but rugged S-38 had
excellent climbing power and a unique wing-
and-tail structure that was attached
to the fuselage by connecting struts.*

HANDLEY PAGE H.P.42E(1931)—IMPERIAL AIRWAYS
*Slow and majestic, the big Handley Page
biplane set new standards of safety and
comfort, including the first sound-insulating
passenger compartments.*

JUNKERS JU 52/3M(1932)—DEUTSCHE LUFT HANSA
*With its angled lines, the Ju 52/3m was
the last example of "tin box" aerodynamic
design. Virtually indestructible, it was the
workhorse of the Luftwaffe in World War II.*

BOEING 247D(1934)—UNITED AIR LINES
*With their stressed-skin fuselages
and retractable landing gear, the planes
of Boeing's revolutionary 247 series
were the first of the modern airliners.*

DOUGLAS DC-3(1936)—WESTERN AIRLINES
*The DC-3, the most widely used passenger
aircraft of its era, incorporated the snub-
nosed prow and swept-back wings that
would characterize most airliners for decades
to come. Its wing flaps reduced landing
speed to a safe and comfortable 64 mph.*

4

Evolution of the plane that transformed air travel

Hearing the engines sputter and die above him, Edward Baker looked to the cloud-filled sky over his father's Kansas farm and saw a large airliner falling heavily to earth, shedding a wing as it came. Seconds later, the plane slammed into the Baker cow pasture with such force that one of its engines was completely buried in the ground. Joined by a field hand from a neighboring farm, young Baker rushed toward the wreckage. There were no signs of life; all seven men on board had died on impact.

The crash, on March 31, 1931, was news throughout the country, because one of the victims was Knute Rockne, the famous Notre Dame football coach. But the significance of the event extended beyond the front pages. The plane, operated by TWA, was a 10-passenger Fokker Trimotor, a model widely used by United States airlines because of its dependability and pleasing design. But government investigators, after weeks of probing the wreckage, reported that they had found evidence of structural weakness that had caused the craft to come apart in mid-air. Inside the huge wooden wing—a massive affair with spars and ribs of spruce enclosed in layers of thin veneer—there were unmistakable signs of rot.

The government ordered all Fokkers inspected regularly against a recurrence of the disaster, but the meticulous procedure was too expensive for TWA; buying new planes might be cheaper. Jack Frye, who was then the airline's director of operations, grounded the Fokkers and began shopping around for a replacement. Frye was soon joined in his search by executives from other airlines. Their inquiries would have a profound influence on future aircraft design, setting in motion a chain of events that accelerated the shift from wood to metal construction and helped bring into being the fast and efficient planes that would soon dominate the air lanes.

Like all sweeping changes, the so-called airframe revolution could come about only when conditions were ripe—when powerful engines and high-octane fuels were available, when aluminum alloys were improved, and when devices such as wing flaps and variable pitch propellers had been fully tested. When those conditions had been met design-

A glistening fleet of DC-3s takes shape on Douglas Aircraft's production line in 1936. Less than a year after its 1935 debut, the DC-3 had outperformed all rivals and was in high demand.

ers could put the pieces together to change the way men might fly.

As early as World War I, a handful of innovative designers had begun to find ways to eliminate the cumbersome wing bracing of struts and guy wires that created so much drag on early aircraft. Their work had produced the first airframe breakthroughs. One of these thinkers was the German aeronautical scientist Hugo Junkers, who designed a cantilevered wing, braced internally with metal spars and covered with corrugated metal; it needed no external support.

Junkers first used this new type of construction in a wartime fighter plane. In 1919 he adapted it to an all-metal, low-wing airliner, the F-13. While Junkers' first metal warplanes had been made of steel and were thus too heavy to be practical, the F-13 was built of the aluminum alloy duralumin, which was almost as light as aluminum and more than twice as strong.

Despite all its sturdiness, the corrugated covering designed by Junkers had its disadvantages. Like an accordion pleat, its strength lay only in the direction of its ridges, and both wings and fuselage required heavy internal bracing in order to keep them rigid under the buffeting stresses encountered in flight. The corrugations also hindered the free passage of air and created drag.

Another influential German designer, Adolf K. Rohrbach, came up with an ingenious solution to these problems when he stretched duralumin sheeting over a light but rigid metal framework so that it resisted stresses from every direction while presenting a smooth, streamlined exterior. Rohrbach's stressed-skin construction was so strong it was almost self-bracing. A wing using his design consisted of a series of boxlike duralumin girders over which the metal skin was tightly bound; a fuselage built in the same manner required almost no interior bracing, thus saving both space and weight.

What Junkers and Rohrbach did with metal, Anthony Fokker sought to accomplish with lighter-weight wood. In a number of military craft he designed for the Germans during World War I and in a series of successful high-wing transport planes he built later, after immigrating to the United States, the young designer constructed cantilevered wings with wooden braces and a plywood covering. His fuselages were of welded steel tubing, covered with fabric or plywood. Although Fokker's reliance on wood brought his F-10 Trimotor to grief in the Knute Rockne crash, his basic design ideas strongly influenced other innovators.

Borrowing from these European pioneers, the engaging American engineer and idea man William B. Stout had been tinkering with some of the same concepts. After building an experimental aircraft with a huge cantilevered wing made of wood, he decided to apply the same principles to the construction of a duralumin monoplane transport. Then Henry Ford bought up Stout's company and went on to order refinements in Stout's design. The result was the Ford Tri-motor, or Tin Goose. Similar in fundamental design to the Fokker F-7, but with a skin of corrugated metal in the Junkers manner, the plane became one of

Dutch-born aircraft designer Anthony Fokker (on the right in puttees) conducts business in a Fokker F.VII that served as his traveling office. The first trimotor in the United States, this plane won the 1925 Ford Reliability Tour race. Edsel Ford then bought it to carry explorer Richard Byrd on his 1926 flight to the Arctic.

America's favorite commercial transport planes during the late 1920s.

In an era when large numbers of ordinary citizens were taking to the air for the first time, passengers found the Ford's three engines and all-metal construction reassuring, and the 12-passenger cabin, with its window curtains, cane-backed seats and individual light fixtures, appeared almost luxurious. But there were drawbacks, too. The Tin Goose was noisy—passengers had to shout to be heard while aloft—and it vibrated mercilessly; in winter the cabin temperature hovered around 50°. The craft was also aerodynamically clumsy—as were the Fokker and every other early trimotor. The placement of its three engines—one in the nose and one slung under each wing—created considerable drag. The Ford rarely exceeded a cruising speed of 105 miles per hour. At such slow speeds the public appeal of air travel was relatively limited, and it was almost impossible for any airline flying one of the trimotors to survive without a mail contract.

A few farsighted airline executives were beginning to sense that such lumbering transports would never make money. What the airlines needed, they felt, were economical planes that could carry passengers swiftly and comfortably to their destinations. But neither engine makers nor aeronautical designers yet knew just how to fashion such a plane. They would soon learn. And when they did, a small band of innovators in the United States building upon the past work of European designers, would take the world lead in aircraft design.

John K. "Jack" Northrop was nine years old when he moved with his family from Nebraska to Santa Barbara, California, in 1904. He took an early interest in aviation, and after graduating from Santa Barbara High School—where he had honed a natural knack for geometry and mechanical drawing—he went to work in 1916 for the Loughead brothers, Allan and Malcolm, who were building a seven-seat flying boat in the corner of an automobile repair shop. (Later, to avoid being called "Loghead," the Lougheads would change the spelling of their name to the phonetically correct Lockheed.)

The Lockheed concern soon received a contract to build flying boats for the United States Navy, and Northrop stayed with the brothers until 1920, when they went broke in the face of competition from thousands of war-surplus Army aircraft that were thrown onto the civilian market. For a time, he worked for his father, a building contractor; then he signed on with Donald Douglas, an up-and-coming plane manufacturer in nearby Santa Monica. In 1926, Northrop worked in his spare time to put together an imaginative design that was far different from the conventional craft that Douglas was building at the time. Deciding that he wanted to own a piece of the company that built the new plane, Northrop got together again with the Lockheeds and helped them launch a second Lockheed Aircraft Company.

The new company's first airplane, based on Northrop's design, was a four-passenger, high-wing monoplane with a highly respectable cruising speed of 135 miles per hour. Dubbed the Lockheed Vega, the single-engined craft combined Anthony Fokker's internally braced wooden wing with an adaptation of Adolf Rohrbach's fuselage scheme in which the exterior skin carries the bulk of the entire load, much as an eggshell does. The plane was not widely used by the airlines, but it would be made famous by the likes of Wiley Post, who flew his Vega, the *Winnie Mae,* around the world in the summer of 1931, and Amelia Earhart, who flew a Vega in her nonstop solo flight across the Atlantic Ocean in May 1932.

With its trim silhouette and smooth-skinned surface, the Vega was one of the first streamlined commercial aircraft in the world. And after the first few models Northrop was able to make it even more aerodynamically efficient when he increased the plane's cruising speed to 155 miles per hour by enclosing the radial Pratt & Whitney Wasp engine in a smooth metal cowl.

Previously, radial engines had been left uncovered. They were air-cooled, after all, and it was reasonable to assume that they would need maximum ventilation. Then, in 1928, an engineer named Fred E. Weick, working for the government's National Advisory Committee for Aeronautics, confirmed that cowling the engine would eliminate much of the drag that was bedeviling radial-engined craft. To assure ample airflow for cooling it was only necessary to leave the cowl open at the front and rear.

The NACA cowl was of little value on radial engines that were hung below the wings of a multiengined plane such as the Ford Tri-motor. The positioning of such power plants created more air resistance than could be overcome with even the most streamlined cowling. But Weick found that if the cowled engines were set into the wing itself, mounted in podlike housings known as nacelles, they gained tremendously in efficiency. The Vega, being single-engined, was not affected by this discovery, and the Ford's form could not be altered. But it was a finding of great importance to future aircraft designs.

Northrop left Lockheed in 1928 to go out on his own and followed up the Vega in 1930 with the single-engined Northrop Alpha, a craft that was still more advanced. A low-wing monoplane intended for use as a mail and passenger carrier by TWA, the Alpha was made entirely of metal and incorporated the design principles of Adolf Rohrbach to an unprecedented degree. Not only did Northrop cover the plane with stressed-skin duralumin, but he improved on Rohrbach's box-spar wing by working out his own method of internal multicellular construction, consisting of aluminum spars and ribs that formed a series of small, rigid compartments, or cells, much like those of a honeycomb. The Alpha's wing was extremely light, yet it was one of the strongest and most resilient in all of aviation.

Northrop was not the only American disciple of Adolf Rohrbach. The German designer's radical ideas were also spreading to some of the bigger manufacturers. A craft similar to the Alpha was produced in 1930

A woman boards a Junkers F-13 airliner in the 1920s by means of steps built into its corrugated duralumin wing. More than 300 of the pioneer all-metal planes were built between 1919 and 1932 at the Junkers aircraft plant in Dessau, Germany.

by Seattle's Boeing Airplane Company. Like the Alpha, the Boeing Monomail was an all-metal, stressed-skin, low-wing monoplane that could cruise at 135 miles per hour. Its rounded fuselage was similar to that of the Alpha, and of the Vega before it. Most notably, Boeing's brilliant chief designer, Claire Egtvedt, had reduced drag even more by a mechanism that pulled the Monomail's landing gear up into the wing after takeoff. Retractable landing gear had been used on amphibians and racing planes for years, but as long as transport speeds hovered around 110 miles per hour designers had felt that the additional weight of the apparatus was not worth the slight gain in air speed. With aircraft becoming faster, however, any reduction in drag was worth attempting, and tests showed that retracting the wheels increased air speed by 6 to 8 per cent.

Egtvedt followed up the Monomail in 1931 with a twin-engined adaptation, considerably larger but embodying the same sleek lines, and entered it in an Army Air Corps competition for the selection of a new bomber. Called the B-9, the plane could fly at 186 miles per hour, not only faster than any previous American bomber but also faster than most pursuit planes of the day. One reason for its impressive performance was the way in which the engines were mounted, protruding well out in front of the wing's leading edge. Further NACA tests on engine cowlings had shown that if an engine were placed in this position there would be less airflow interference between the propeller and the wing itself, and the plane would have more power.

Despite its many superior qualities, the B-9 did not win the competition; the Air Corps chose instead a still faster plane built by another manufacturer, the Glenn L. Martin Company. But by that time Boeing was at work on a new transport plane that the company was sure would revolutionize air travel. This latest plane was an outgrowth of both the Monomail and the B-9 and it was designed to incorporate all the structural and aerodynamic advances used in those aircraft: cantilevered all-metal wings, stressed-skin construction, retractable landing gear, and wing-mounted engines with cowlings—though the partial cowling system chosen by Boeing was somewhat less efficient than the NACA design. Powered by a pair of 600-horsepower Pratt & Whitney Hornet engines, the 10-passenger plane was intended to be the most powerful and fastest airliner in the skies. Boeing officials were confident that this dream plane, designated the 247, would make their company the nation's premier manufacturer of commercial aircraft.

The 247 was still in the early stages of production—though its general specifications were well known in the aviation industry—when TWA's Jack Frye launched his search for a successor to the Fokker

The exceptionally modern, clean lines of this Lockheed Vega belie the fact that the plane was designed in 1927. Vegas were among the first planes to have the special drag-reducing engine cowl developed by the National Advisory Committee for Aeronautics in the late 1920s.

Trimotors. But when the young executive inquired about buying some of the new planes, he was informed that the entire projected output of sixty 247s was already earmarked for the four commercial air carriers owned by Boeing's parent organization, United Aircraft and Transport, and known together as United Air Lines. Once United's order had been filled—in a couple of years—Frye could come back and see about buying 247s for TWA.

Frye could not wait that long, and he sought out bids from other manufacturers. From one of them, Douglas Aircraft of Santa Monica, California, he received a reply that would change aviation history.

Donald Wills Douglas, the founder of Douglas Aircraft, had never built a large transport plane. But he was hardly a newcomer to aeronautics. Indeed, he had been building top-rated military planes for more than a decade. The son of a bank cashier of Scottish descent, Douglas was born and raised in Brooklyn, New York. When he was in his teens, his great love was sailing, and he followed an older brother's footsteps to the United States Naval Academy.

But by the time young Douglas arrived at Annapolis in 1909 he was already shifting his sights. The year before, on a visit to Washington, he had gone to nearby Fort Myer, Virginia, to watch Orville Wright demonstrate his pusher plane for the Army. From that moment, Douglas was smitten with the idea of flight. After three years at Annapolis he made his decision: He would transfer to the Massachusetts Institute of Technology and become an aeronautical engineer. He was told by M.I.T. that it would take him four years to complete the course; he graduated with distinction in two.

Douglas worked for a time as a teaching assistant in M.I.T.'s new aeronautical engineering department, then got a job with a Connecticut company that was building the United States Navy's first dirigible. In 1915 the pioneer aviator Glenn Martin, who was building seaplanes on the West Coast, heard of Douglas' talents and sent for him to join his company as chief engineer. Arriving in Los Angeles, the 23-year-old Douglas was met at his hotel by Martin, who sputtered: "Why, you're just a boy. A boy engineer."

"I think he had the idea," Douglas recalled later, "that anybody who came out of M.I.T. would have a long beard."

At the Martin Company, Douglas soon found that his engineering talents were badly needed. The firm's methods were extremely unscientific; one day Martin climbed into the cockpit of a seaplane whose floats were resting on sawhorses and then began to throw his weight back and forth and up and down. Douglas asked him what he was doing. "I'm testing it, to see if it's strong enough," replied Martin. Not long afterward, Douglas announced that he would require detailed drawings for each new design and that he would subject all of its components to stress analysis before construction got under way. Other employees scoffed at the move, but Martin supported his young engineer.

Douglas left Martin in 1916 and went to work for the Aviation Section of the Army Signal Corps in Washington, but a little more than a year later he resigned out of exasperation with government red tape. Glenn Martin, by this time operating in Cleveland, was glad to have him back. By 1920, however, Douglas was ready to cut loose and start his own company. With less than $1,000 in savings, he returned to Southern California; he had come to like the area and wanted to set up shop in a location that was suitable for year-round flying.

It was a bad time to launch an aircraft company in any location. Military buying had dried up with the postwar demobilization, there was little commercial flying yet and the United States economy was teetering on the verge of a recession. Douglas tried fruitlessly to raise money. Then a friend introduced him to David Davis, a well-to-do young Californian who wanted to build a plane to fly nonstop coast to coast. The two men formed the Davis-Douglas Company and rented a single

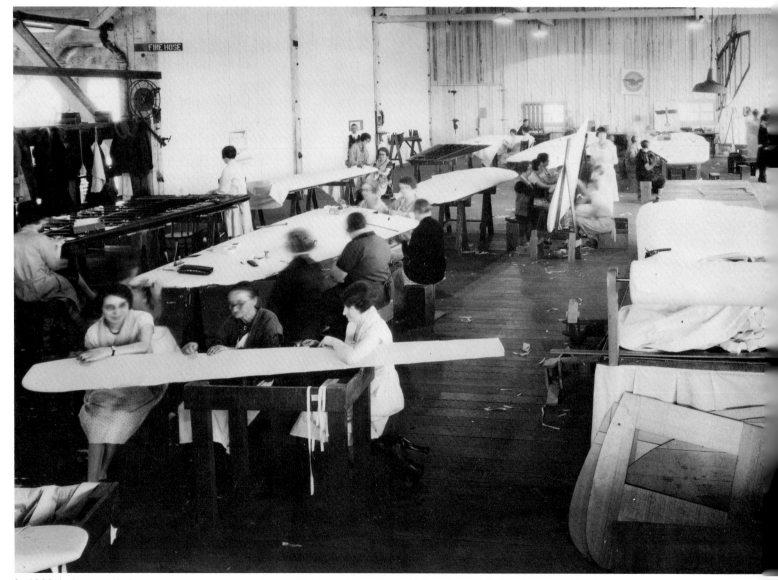

In 1928, before metal planes were common, seamstresses attach fabric to wing and tail sections at the Boeing assembly plant.

room in the rear of a barber shop; not long afterward they moved to the loft of a Los Angeles planing mill. Douglas bought a $25 electric hand drill—the new concern's first equipment purchase—and made use of woodworking machinery from the mill. He also persuaded a handful of former Martin comrades to come out from Cleveland to join him. Presently he built a sturdy biplane, called the Cloudster, for Davis' transcontinental flight. The Cloudster had a unique distinction: It was the first airplane ever built anywhere that could lift a payload exceeding its own weight.

The Cloudster's engine failed on the plane's way across the country, and Davis made a forced landing at Fort Bliss, Texas. By the time he was ready for a second try, a Fokker T-2 flown by two Army officers had already accomplished the nonstop transcontinental feat; Davis then lost interest in the project and withdrew from the company.

Douglas, meanwhile, had gone to Washington and convinced the Navy that he could build an effective torpedo bomber based on the Cloudster design. With Navy funds in his pocket, he was able to persuade a number of Los Angeles investors to put their money into his newly renamed Douglas Company. The Navy bought the bomber from Douglas, and the company's star rose still higher in 1924 when three of its so-called World Cruisers, built for the Army, made a widely publicized circumnavigation of the globe. By then, Douglas had outgrown its loft and moved to more spacious quarters in an abandoned movie studio in Santa Monica.

Aside from building the highly successful M-series mailplanes and a twin-engined flying boat called the Dolphin, Douglas in the late 1920s and early 1930s concentrated on military orders. By 1929 the company had moved to still larger quarters adjacent to Clover Field, an airport in Santa Monica. At about the same time, Donald Douglas set up a useful liaison with Pasadena's California Institute of Technology. In 1932 he was rejoined by the immensely creative Jack Northrop, who had worked for Douglas briefly in the mid-1920s. Northrop's own company had been bought out by the United Aircraft conglomerate and moved to Kansas. Declining to leave California, Northrop resigned and formed a new concern, the Northrop Corporation, as a subsidiary of Douglas Aircraft. Now the marvelous Northrop wing was part of the Douglas arsenal. So it was that in 1932 Douglas Aircraft was solvent, well staffed with gifted designers and ready for the difficult challenge that came from Jack Frye of TWA.

Frye was intent on finding a craft whose performance would equal or outdo the 247's. He wanted the plane's internal structure to be built mainly of metal, he wrote, though some components could be of other materials. The plane would have to weigh no more than 14,200 pounds and it must carry at least 12 passengers. Frye also wanted a speed of 150 miles per hour and a cruising range of at least 1,080 miles. As for power plants, Frye was flexible, though he preferred a trimotor. And to guard against crack-ups if an engine failed during takeoff, he specified further that the plane must be able to get off the ground fully loaded, on any combination of two of its three engines, from any airfield in the TWA system—some of which were several thousand feet above sea level, where the rarefied atmosphere provided less lift. He also demanded a landing speed of 65 miles per hour or less—the same as that of the Ford Tri-motor.

Douglas and his associates were well aware of what their rivals at Boeing were up to, and after some discussion they arrived at two key decisions. First, they would go all out to exceed the TWA specifications, thus further eclipsing the Boeing 247. Second, they would follow Boeing's lead and build a twin-engined plane rather than a trimotor. As chief engineer James H. "Dutch" Kindelberger put it, the Knute Rockne crash had given trimotors a bad name. "Why build anything," he asked, "that even looks like a Fokker or Ford?"

The Douglas engineers resolved that their transport would incorporate the most advanced aircraft-design features then known, among them all-metal stressed-skin construction, NACA engine cowlings and nacelles, and retractable landing gear. And to achieve a landing speed of 65 miles per hour despite the craft's expected high cruising speed, Douglas would employ wing flaps, which had been used for some years on smaller planes but never on a big transport. When lowered, the flaps would increase the wings' camber, or curvature, thus producing more lift and thereby permitting slower landings while improving takeoff performance. Finally, the group decided to use a modified version of the multicellular wing construction that Northrop had pioneered in the Alpha. They also picked a name for their new plane. They would call it the DC-1, for Douglas Commercial No. 1.

Just 10 days after Douglas received Frye's inquiry, Kindelberger's assistant, Arthur Raymond, and general manager Harry Wetzel took a train to New York to submit the proposal to TWA. They could have flown, but Raymond needed more time to hone his presentation. By the time the two reached New York they were ready with detailed specifications covering everything from engines and instrument panels to lavatory design and width of the aisle between the seats.

As he described the proposed aircraft to the executives assembled in TWA's office, Raymond's major concern was the demand that the plane be able to take off from any TWA airfield with one engine out. This would not have been so challenging in a trimotor such as Frye had first envisioned, but it would be more difficult in the Douglas twin-engined model. Then TWA's technical adviser, Charles Lindbergh, stiffened the requirement: The new plane must not only meet this rigid takeoff specification, he said, but it must also be capable on a single engine of climbing and maintaining level flight over the highest mountains along any TWA route. Raymond telephoned Donald Douglas in Santa Monica to report this new and unexpected development. He was 90 per cent certain that the plane could do it, he told Douglas. Then he added: "The 10 per cent is keeping me awake nights."

Douglas consulted with Dutch Kindelberger, who replied: "There's only one way to find out. Build the thing and try it." TWA, impressed with the Douglas proposal, agreed to Kindelberger's bold prescription. On September 20, 1932, the airline signed a contract to buy a single test aircraft and took an option to buy as many as 60 more.

As work on the plane got under way, Douglas and his design team began devising still more improvements. The wing, further refined in shape after extensive wind-tunnel tests at Cal Tech, was to be installed in a brand-new way. Instead of being a single unit, it would be built in three sections—a center part, integral with the fuselage and containing engine mounts and landing gear, and two outer wing panels beyond. These outer panels would be held firmly in place by bolts, thus making repairs or replacements simple: If a section was damaged it could easily be unbolted and a new one attached.

The new wing was extraordinarily tough—a characteristic Douglas engineers tested by placing one on the ground and repeatedly driving a steam roller over it. The wing was not even slightly damaged. It was elastic, too, as future passengers would sometimes note with alarm when they saw their aircraft's wings flexing with the stresses of flight. The wing would also have a distinctive appearance by the time the plane was finished. For as work progressed Arthur Raymond found that the plane weighed more than originally planned; with the addition of

A youthful Donald Douglas (left) works at his drafting table, probably in the Martin aircraft company plant in Cleveland (the setting and date of the photograph are uncertain). His most important project for Martin was the giant MB-1 bomber, the only United States-designed combat plane developed during World War I.

weight, the aircraft's center of gravity was moving rearward. Rather than shift the whole wing to the rear to compensate, he swept the leading edges back sharply while keeping the trailing edges straight; seen from below, the result was a unique, almost triangular, swept-back silhouette.

Another major feature—this one suggested by a TWA engineer—was easily demountable engines. All engine lines and fittings were designed so that they could be disconnected directly behind the engine itself, enabling changes to be made swiftly and thus cutting maintenance costs. Passenger comfort was a high priority for the plane's designers, and the craft would have a number of features that in later years would be taken for granted: well-upholstered seats with adjustable backs, adequate heating and ventilation, and thorough soundproofing.

While Douglas was refining plans for its DC-1, Boeing was putting the finishing touches on its own dream plane, the 247. On February 8, 1933, the new all-metal airliner made its first flight, lifting off from Boeing's Seattle test field and winging gracefully over Puget Sound. As the sleek craft was put through its paces, a Boeing engineer was said to have remarked proudly: "They'll never build them any bigger."

In fact, the 247 was not even as big as Boeing's designers had originally intended, nor was it as speedy as first planned. Before starting construction, the manufacturer had asked Boeing Air Transport pilots to comment on the plane's specifications. Conservative by nature, the fliers said the craft would be too heavy and too fast to land safely. So the plans were scaled down; the craft's gross weight was reduced from 16,000 to 12,650 pounds and less powerful 550-horsepower Pratt & Whitney Wasp engines were substituted for the 600-horsepower Hornets originally specified. Even so, the plane's cruising speed of 155 miles per hour made it the fastest airliner then in service. On its first scheduled coast-to-coast passenger run, little more than three months after the first trial flight in Seattle, a 247 made it from San Francisco to New York in just 19½ hours, nearly eight hours less than any previous airliner's time. But its new and formidable challenger from Douglas was soon to take to the skies.

On July 1, 1933, the aluminum-bodied Douglas DC-1 stood glistening in the bright California sun, poised for its initial flight. To those who were seeing it for the first time, the plane seemed enormous, as indeed it was by the standards of the day. Its 85-foot wingspan was 11 feet wider than the 247's; at 60 feet in length the DC-1 was almost nine feet longer than the Boeing airliner. And the new plane weighed in at 17,500 pounds, 4,850 pounds more than the 247.

To power this big aircraft, Douglas engineers had installed a pair of 710-horsepower Wright Cyclone engines and fitted them with newly refined variable pitch propellers. Now pilots could adjust propeller-blade angles at will, making it possible to set them for maximum efficiency at both high and low speeds.

Donald Douglas and hundreds of his employees had gathered on

A Douglas Aircraft employee drives a steam roller over a wing designed for the original DC-1. "The structure never gave an inch," boasted manufacturer Donald Douglas, who required rugged testing of all DC-1 parts before the assembly of the prototype airplane in 1933.

Dozens of 80-pound shot bags are heaped onto the movable airfoil, or aileron, of a DC-1 wing to check its performance under extreme pressure. This and other ground tests ordered by Douglas were designed to simulate the stress the airplane would experience in severe flight conditions.

their lunch hour to watch their creation test its wings. Test pilot Carl A. Cover, wearing a tweed suit and a bright green hat, taxied the plane to the far end of Clover Field, gunned the engines and roared down the runway. As the plane lifted from the ground, Donald Douglas looked at his watch. It was exactly 12:36. Then Douglas looked up and saw that the plane's nose was dipping sharply. "Half a minute later," he recalled afterward, "the port engine sputtered, then quit."

Cover instantly threw the wheel to the right and went into a steep bank, narrowly missing a tree. As the nose went down, the engine sprang to life, but when the pilot steadied the craft and resumed climbing, both engines cut out. Donald Douglas heard someone in the nearby crowd exclaim: "She's going to crash!" But Cover pushed the wheel forward to drop the nose, and the engines throbbed into action once more. With consummate skill, he continued to climb—dropping the nose to restart the engines each time they sputtered and died—until he had enough altitude to return to the field.

After touching down to a bumpy landing, Cover taxied up to the transfixed crowd, cut the ignition and made his way out of the craft, a look of puzzlement on his face. Mechanics swarmed over the plane to remove the easily demountable engines, and after several days of painstaking examination they had the answer. The floats in the Cyclone engines' experimental carburetors had been improperly designed, so that as the engines tipped back during a climb, the fuel supply was cut off. The floats were fixed and the trouble disappeared.

Further tests showed that the DC-1 was living up to nearly all expectations. The plane climbed easily to 22,000 feet, landed at a speed well under 65 miles per hour and was astonishingly strong structurally. One day the assigned crew member failed to lower the wheels for landing, and the craft belly-flopped onto the field and skidded smoothly to a stop—its propeller tips bent from chewing up the runway, but the fuselage unharmed except for a few scratches.

But the tantalizing question of whether the plane could complete a takeoff with a failed engine remained to be answered, and later in the year the DC-1 was flown for this crucial test to TWA's highest airport, at Winslow, Arizona, elevation 4,500 feet. The fuselage was loaded with sandbags to simulate a full payload of 18,000 pounds. Recently developed high-octane fuel filled its tanks. Edmund T. Allen, a Douglas test pilot, was at the controls; the copilot, representing TWA, was the veteran flier D. W. "Tommy" Tomlinson. Just behind them was Franklin R. Collbohm, the Douglas engineer in overall charge of the test, whose chief operational duty was to work the landing-gear crank.

Douglas engineers had devised a flight plan that they hoped would minimize the chances of mishap. At the instant that the plane became airborne, Tomlinson would throttle one engine down to half speed; at the same time, Collbohm would crank up the landing gear. If the takeoff was successful with half of one engine's power gone, Allen would bring the plane back around for a second attempt; this time Tomlinson would cut the engine completely. With everyone in place for the first test run, Allen churned the DC-1 down the field. Not until the heavily loaded aircraft had covered three quarters of the runway did Collbohm sense that the wheels had lifted from the ground. And then Tomlinson, instead of throttling back as planned, calmly reached for the ignition switch and shut off the right engine. As instructed, Collbohm had already begun to raise the landing gear. With half its power gone, the plane was now committed to the air.

Caught by surprise, Allen jammed the remaining engine's throttle forward. The plane shuddered momentarily and then began a slow but steady climb. Finally, at about 8,000 feet—well above the mountains surrounding the airfield—Allen turned to his copilot and asked him for an explanation. "It's this way," replied Tomlinson. "You work for the manufacturer. I work for the customer. I just wanted to see if the old girl is as good as you guys claim she is."

The plane was that, and more. Still on one engine, Allen droned on for 280 miles to Albuquerque, New Mexico. He was on the ground and ready to take off for the return flight to Winslow when a TWA Ford Trimotor that had left Winslow before the DC-1's harrowing lift-off finally touched down at Albuquerque.

Delighted TWA executives placed an initial order for 25 of the craft. But their planes would not be exact copies of the DC-1. For even as the new airliner was being tested, Douglas and his colleagues determined that it was strong enough and powerful enough to be enlarged slightly. So they lengthened the fuselage by two feet, rearranged the interior and put in two more seats—seven on each side of the aisle instead of six, for a total of 14. The resulting production model was called the DC-2; with an improved power plant it was able to cruise at 196 miles per hour, as against the DC-1's 190. Other airlines were also interested in pur-

Comfort in the clouds

When America took the lead in aircraft design in the late 1920s, the interiors of planes changed to keep pace with the so-called airframe revolution. As boxy shapes gave way to sleek, stressed-skin contours, designers stopped creating ornate, Pullman-like interiors *(page 22)* and began moving toward simpler and more functional cabins.

But as fittings became less opulent, passenger comfort increased with innovations such as seats that could be adjusted, reading lights, controlled ventilation and heating. And, for the first time, soundproofing inside the passenger compartment made it possible to converse without shouting.

Wicker seats offer little comfort in a Ford Tri-motor in the late 1920s.

A stewardess serves passengers in a Boeing 247 in 1933. Steps cross a wing spar blocking the aisle of this first modern-style cabin.

Passengers stretch out in comfort in a deluxe chair-car version of the DC-3. The extra-fare plane was used on the New York-Chicago run in 1937 and carried 14 rather than the usual 21 passengers.

A secretary takes dictation while fellow passengers read in one of the partitioned sections of a Douglas Sleeper Transport. At night (inset), the seats in each section converted into lower berths, while upper berths folded down from the ceiling.

chasing the craft, and Douglas geared up for increased production.

The single DC-1, the only one ever made, was used only for demonstrations and tests and was never put into regular service. But it did enjoy one moment of public triumph. In February 1934, when the government canceled civilian airmail contracts and turned mail carrying over to the Army, TWA's Jack Frye and his friend Eddie Rickenbacker of Eastern Air Lines got together to stage a dramatic display of commercial aviation's capabilities. The night before the cancellation took effect, the two men flew the TWA DC-1 with a full load of mail from Burbank, California, to Newark, New Jersey. Passing through rough winter weather and making only two refueling stops, they made the transcontinental hop in a record-setting 13 hours and 4 minutes. Wrote one New York newspaper of the feat: "This plane has made obsolete all other air transport equipment in this country or any other." Indeed, the DC-1's successor, the DC-2, would soon turn in a performance that would make the Douglas commercial aircraft known the world over.

Dutch designer Anthony Fokker, whose Trimotor's well-publicized misfortune had helped bring Douglas into the transport business, had been so impressed by the DC-1 that he wangled European sales rights to the DC-2. One of his first customers was KLM Royal Dutch Airlines, which put the planes into service between Amsterdam and the Dutch East Indies. Then, in October of 1934, KLM entered one of its DC-2s in a widely heralded air race from Mildenhall, England, near London, to Melbourne, Australia.

Among the other entrants from many nations were three specially built British de Havilland racers and a Boeing 247, which was flown by two racing pilots. While competitors were required to make only four specified refueling stops along the way, KLM boldly announced that its plane would fly its normal route, 1,000 miles longer than that followed by the other planes, and would also carry passengers plus 30,000 letters. The race came to a stunning finish: The DC-2 handily beat all other transport planes and was bested only by one of the de Havilland racers. The Boeing 247 came in a distant third. KLM's American-built airliner had flown to Melbourne from Mildenhall in less than four days; Imperial Airways, when it began a few months later to serve a similar route with British-built planes, took 12 days to complete the flight. European airline executives suddenly realized how far behind they were. Douglas had led the way to a new age of commercial aviation.

In the United States, too, the DC-2 was outpacing all other contenders. TWA took delivery of the first new plane in May of 1934, and inaugurated speedy coast-to-coast service in August; the line's advertising boasted that the trip took only "18 hours via 200-mile-an-hour luxury airliners." On every run, the DC-2 reached its destination more quickly than the Boeing 247s operated by United. The Douglas craft was more comfortable, too, for Boeing engineers had chosen to run their main wing spar right through the cabin, above the level of the floor, and passengers moving up and down the aisle had to clamber over this annoying hurdle. The Boeing company tried to upgrade the 247 to equal the DC-2, but it was a losing battle; Boeing eventually gave up the struggle and concentrated on building military aircraft. United, saddled with a fleet of outmoded planes, was plunged into gloom as competitors put more and more of the popular DC-2s into service. And even then the triumph of the Douglas commercial airliner was not yet complete.

One day in late 1934, Donald Douglas received a telephone call from C. R. Smith, the crusty and outspoken president of American Airlines. Smith had already ordered some DC-2s, but now he said he needed another kind of plane—a fast sleeper craft that could replace the lumbering Curtiss Condors with which American was inadequately serving its long transcontinental route. And he had a hunch the DC-2 could be widened to hold sleeping berths.

Douglas was not excited by the prospect. "We can't even keep up with the orders for the DC-2s," he protested. But Smith was not the kind of man to give up easily; he stayed on the phone, arguing and cajoling. He even promised to buy 20 of the planes sight unseen, though American had no cash reserves on hand and Smith had no idea where he could get the money. Douglas at last relented and said he would start design studies, and Smith dispatched one of his engineers to Santa Monica to help work out the deails. The brash airline president then journeyed to Washington, where he managed to get a government loan to pay for the planes; Douglas, meanwhile, set out to produce the plane that in time would transform air travel throughout the world.

For the resulting Douglas Sleeper Transport, or DST, turned out to be just a passing phase. Its widened fuselage provided room for 14 berths, and Smith was happy to put the new night plane into service in June 1936—but meanwhile someone had noticed that the same interior would now hold 21 seats, up from the DC-2's 14. Refitted as a day plane, the new craft was called the DC-3.

Even though it was seemingly just a scaled-up version of the DC-2, the Three, as pilots called it, was a significantly different and better airplane. Its retractable landing gear was hydraulically operated (the DC-2's had to be pumped up and down by hand) and fitted with improved shock absorbers, and its adjustable props were of a more advanced design. Far more important was the DC-3's new aerodynamic profile. Douglas engineers had found that enlarging the fuselage—and the resulting need to widen the wingspan by 10 feet—made a plane that was at first unstable. So the wing had to be redesigned, and after exhaustive wind-tunnel tests the Douglas designers came up with wings that were thinner than the DC-2's, particularly at the tips.

The result of these changes was virtual aerodynamic perfection: The DC-3 was so easy to handle that it was said that the craft could almost fly by itself. Pilots quickly noted the difference. The Two was known as "a stiff-legged brute" that was hard to land. But in the words of pilot-writer Ernest Gann, who flew both craft, the Three was "an amiable cow that was forgiving of the most clumsy pilot.'' Air travelers appreciated the added comfort and safety of the plane, and the DC-3 soon became the standard against which other airliners were measured.

For the airlines, the increase in payload from 14 to 21 passengers brought an economic bonanza. The DC-3 was the first plane ever built that could pay its way with passengers alone, and operators no longer had to rely on airmail contracts to turn a profit. The happy combination of higher speed and more passengers meant that the cost per seat-mile dropped radically. (Seat-mile is an airline-industry term for the number of passenger seats flown per mile. A fully occupied 21-seat aircraft that completes a 100-mile flight is said to have flown 2,100 seat-miles.)

Smith's gamble in ordering the new Douglas planes for American paid off richly, for the DC-3 would spark his line's rapid rise to the No. 1 position among domestic air carriers. Other airlines—including the laggard United—soon followed Smith's lead, and by 1939 a full 75 per cent of the nation's air travelers were being carried by DC-3s. Donald Douglas, too, had been rewarded for his bold move: His company soon became one of America's largest makers of aircraft.

The fact that more than half the airliners pictured here at Chicago's municipal airport in the late 1930s are DC-3s indicates the rapid acceptance won by the Douglas planes within a few years of their introduction. By 1940 DC-3s had flown 100 million miles and had carried nearly 3 million passengers.

With the coming of the DC-3, the airframe revolution was complete, and the modern airliner had arrived. Except for the introduction in the 1940s of pressurized cabins for high-altitude flight and tricycle landing gear that enabled planes to stand in a level position rather than with their tails down, there would be no major changes in commercial aircraft design until the advent of the passenger jets some 20 years later. Propeller-driven planes would become larger and faster and would fly with four engines instead of two, but they would remain basically the same as the DC-3.

But if the DC-3 had ended a revolution, it had also started something else—its own legend. The plane's strength and resilience made it seem all but indestructible, and soon after it arrived on the airways amazing stories—many of them true—began to accumulate about the DC-3. One flying from Chicago to Detroit hit a downdraft so severe that several seats were ripped from the floor, a number of seat belts snapped and passengers were tossed around in the cabin. But after the pilot regained control of the plane and landed, the craft was thoroughly inspected and found to have not one loose rivet or any other sign of damage.

Another DC-3, on its way from Atlanta to Chicago, flew into a cold front and rapidly began accumulating ice on its wings and in its carburetors as well. The pilot cleared the carburetors by causing the engines to backfire repeatedly, endured updrafts and downdrafts that flung the plane from 5,000 feet to 13,000 feet and back down again, and eventually guided the craft to an emergency landing at Indianapolis after breaking the ice-caked windshield with a fire extinguisher so that he could see where he was going. Looking over the plane on the ground he found on the wings and tail a two-inch layer of solid ice that must have weighed a ton or more.

A third DC-3, involved in a mid-air collision with another craft, lost five feet from the end of one wing, including part of an aileron; its pilot brought it down in a nearby field with no trouble.

Later, the DC-3 would perform yeoman service during World War II, when military-transport versions were known in the United States Army as the C-47, in the Navy as the R4D and in Britain's Royal Air Force as the Dakota. And while Douglas would stop making the DC-3 soon after the War, the hardy plane was to live on. Thousands that had been built for military use were converted into civilian airliners and put into service on the scheduled airlines or as nonscheduled carriers.

Of the nearly 11,000 DC-3s and military equivalents Douglas made, hundreds would still be in service even into the 1980s. The all-time champion appears to be a craft that logged more than 50,000 hours in the air for Eastern Air Lines after its delivery in 1939. In 1952 it was sold to North Central Airlines and flew until 1965, when it was retired from regular service. By the time it was donated later to the Henry Ford Museum in Dearborn, Michigan, the plane had flown for nearly 85,000 hours, the equivalent of almost 10 full years in the air. In the process, it had worn out 550 tires, 25,000 spark plugs and 136 engines.   ➳

Tender loving care aloft

The sheer novelty of flying could enthrall air passengers only briefly before familiar concerns—hunger, thirst and boredom—reasserted themselves. European airlines addressed the problem first by hiring cabin boys, uniformed like hotel bellboys and performing similar duties; later, their responsibilities were upgraded to resemble those of a ship's steward.

It was in America, however, that an airline executive, United's S. A. "Steve" Simpson, first proposed adding a woman, a registered nurse, to each aircrew. "Imagine the psychology," he said in a 1930 memo to a superior. "Imagine the tremendous effect on the traveling public." An answering telegram of one word—NO—was countermanded after further negotiation, and Ellen Church, who had suggested the idea to Simpson, was hired to recruit single nurses under 25 years of age.

But stewardesses of the 1930s were not yet the glamorous symbols of adventure they were to become. Their duties were to bolt the seats to the floor before each flight, offer cotton for passengers' ears to muffle noise, make sure the passengers chose the door to the toilet instead of the nearby emergency exit, warn against throwing lighted cigar butts out the window and "carry a railroad timetable in case the plane is grounded somewhere."

One of the first flight attendants, Jack Sanderson, 14, assists a passenger from the cabin of a British Daimler Airway plane in 1922. Sanderson died in a crash in 1923.

A steward serves lunch on Luft Hansa's Berlin-to-Vienna express, which in the late 1920s became the first airline to provide hot meals.

The first stewardesses (led by Ellen Church, upper left) model the caped United uniforms they wore when they began work in May of 1930.

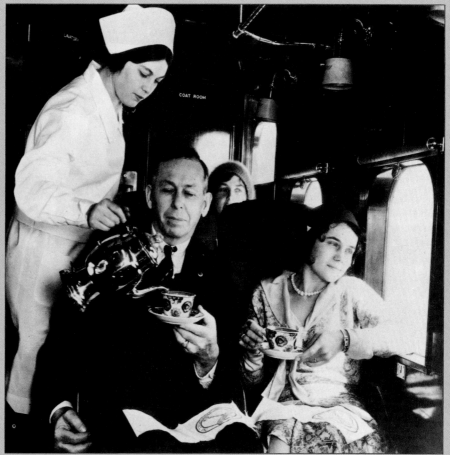

Dressed to reflect her nursing qualifications, an early stewardess serves coffee.

Four 1936 stewardesses unsolemnly swear not to end their careers by marrying—yet.

Stewardesses in 1939 line up in front of a United Air Lines DC-3 to introduce a more stylish look to their growing profession.

5

The man who shrank the earth

On the afternoon of November 22, 1935, a multitude descended on the shores of San Francisco Bay to swarm over docks, rooftops and the decks of every available ferry. On the flag-draped pier in Alameda stood Postmaster General James Farley and scores of local dignitaries facing the world's most advanced flying boat, which was bobbing peacefully at anchor.

Over an international radio hookup Farley read a congratulatory message from President Franklin D. Roosevelt. Then, as rockets burst, boat whistles shrilled and 170 Boy Scouts displayed an enormous American flag, messages were radioed from island bases in the Pacific. "Pan American Airways ocean air base No. 1, Honolulu, Hawaii, standing by for orders," "Midway standing by for orders"—and so on from Wake, Guam and the Philippines. All was ready for the inauguration of the first scheduled transpacific airmail service. A tall, broad-faced man stepped to the microphone to address the pilot: "Captain Musick, you have your sailing orders," he said. "Cast off and depart for Manila in accordance therewith." A band burst into "The Star-Spangled Banner" as the flying boat lifted off from the water and banked west for Hawaii.

The man at the microphone was Juan Terry Trippe, creator of an aerial empire that soon would girdle the globe. Of all the airline builders of the 1920s and 1930s, he was perhaps the most remarkable, for he understood the enormous potential of international flight and, starting with a fledgling company, had built a phenomenally successful carrier while United States domestic airlines were still hesitantly trying their wings. To those who knew him, the ceremony that sent Pan American's fabled *China Clipper* speeding across the Pacific was at once inspiring and predictable. For if Trippe stood at the summit of commercial aviation on that day in 1935, it was because his vision was matched by extraordinary courage, tenacity and ambition. And if the ceremony itself breathed patriotic fervor, it was because Juan Trippe—and others as well—linked the fortunes of Pan American Airways to the overseas economic and political interests of the United States.

To a world struggling out of economic depression, Trippe's great gleaming flying boats, winging their way to distant shores, symbolized

The Philippine Clipper descends over Hong Kong harbor in this watercolor commemorating Pan American's first commercial flight linking the United States and China on October 23, 1936.

not only elegance and luxury but adventure and romance to a degree never quite equaled since. Overseas, they were indeed standard bearers for America—tangible testimony to the power and benevolent will of a nation that few foreigners had experienced directly. In time, Pan American was to become almost a department of state in itself. Borrowing a phrase from British diplomacy, federal bureaucrats sometimes referred to it as a "chosen instrument"—implying that its interests paralleled those of the national government, which was justified, therefore, in giving it virtual monopoly powers. As it prospered, it raised again in altered terms questions about the relationship of airlines to government that had been largely dormant since the stormy days of Postmaster General Walter Folger Brown, who had imperiously awarded airmail contracts and consolidated routes in a manner many private carriers regarded as dictatorial.

Pan American Airways, wrote an early student of the company, was "put together by rich men with a feeling in the seat of their pants for flying." Substantially, he was correct. One vice president in the early years amused himself by computing the combined wealth of the young men with such names as Vanderbilt, Whitney, Harriman and Lehman he saw around the board-room table: He was amazed, he later recalled, to arrive at a figure of about $850 million. Juan Trippe's own inherited wealth was modest by comparison—he was the son of a New York investment banker—but the assets of initiative and imagination he brought to the new company were matched by nobody else at the table.

The man who liked to stress that his airline was "100 per cent American" had acquired a Spanish name—which later opened doors for him in Latin America—because his mother was fond of an aunt called Juanita. In fact, Trippe detested the name Juan—though he never cultivated a nickname to supplant it—and was proud of his descent from English seafarers who had come to Maryland in the 17th Century. At private school and at Yale he was a shy, unassertive young man who spoke politely, earned indifferent grades and made scant impression on his classmates. In 1917 he left Yale to become a Navy bomber pilot, and though he saw no action, he returned to campus so hooked on aviation that he founded a collegiate flying club. On graduation he showed that there was something tough and curiously daring behind the bland exterior: Resisting family pressure to take up a more conventional career, he resolved to make his way in the perilous world of aviation.

His chance came when he learned that seven war-surplus Navy seaplanes were being auctioned off at the Philadelphia Navy Yard. Young Trippe entered a bid of $500 apiece, got the planes and in 1923 launched a charter service ferrying socialites to resort areas. Even at that early stage of his career, he foresaw, as few other people did, that aviation would soon cease to be a diversion and would become a major means of public transport. He haunted the New York Public Library studying the operations of other kinds of carriers—railroads, buses,

A youthful Juan Trippe displays the powerful physique that won him a place on the 1917 Yale football team. The future Pan Am president had already started earning his wings with a stint at the Curtiss Flying School in Miami that summer.

shipping lines—and he demonstrated a shrewd ability to use personal contacts that would characterize him throughout his career. He spent much of his time in the offices of concerns such as the United Fruit Company and the Pennsylvania Railroad Company, talking about operating costs with executives he had met through college friends.

The charter service failed in late 1924, after a number of the planes were wrecked and competition in the resort trade became so intense it ceased to be profitable. Shortly thereafter Congress passed the Kelly Act authorizing airmail payments to private contractors. Seeking out some of his wealthy Yale friends—among them socialite Cornelius Vanderbilt "Sonny" Whitney—Trippe founded a paper organization called Eastern Air Transport (the same name was later used by another company that ultimately became Eastern Air Lines). He then began lobbying diligently for the New York-Boston contract. When confronted with a rival bidder, Colonial Airways, he contrived a merger. Colonial bagged the contract and Trippe became the line's managing director.

Although Colonial was a substantial operation, it was not big enough for Juan Trippe. He bought two Ford and two Fokker trimotors and began plotting ambitious route extensions. On a flight to Havana with Tony Fokker, he obtained with characteristic foresight what he later described as "a simple two- or three-page letter" in which Cuban President Gerardo Machado granted Trippe personally a number of concessions—including exclusive landing rights—essential to any airline proposing to fly to Cuba. Already, Trippe confided in a letter to a friend, he was thinking of carrying the mail from Key West to Havana.

Nobody doubted his capacity for work. Rarely seen at social functions—and then usually as his sister's escort —he spent his spare time at Hadley Field near New Brunswick, New Jersey, quizzing mail pilots about problems on their routes. But the Colonial board was disconcerted: They thought Trippe was moving too far and too fast. He thought they were "a bunch of old fogies." Within 18 months he was out.

Undismayed, he recruited Whitney and the others once again and in June 1927 formed a new company with the resounding title of Aviation Corporation of America. He had his eye not only on the Key West-Havana franchise but on one for the whole of South America, where no United States airline flew.

The problem was that two other outfits were interested in flying the mail to Havana. One was a group headed by a New York broker named Richard Hoyt that had operated a now nearly defunct airline in Florida and still had a corporate structure and finances, but no planes. The other was an organization that had been founded largely for patriotic reasons by four Army Air Corps officers—most notably Major Henry H. "Hap" Arnold, who would one day lead the Army Air Forces in World War II. Arnold, an intelligence officer stationed in Washington, was worried about a German-run airline that was operating in Colombia under the acronym SCADTA. Convinced that the Germans posed a potential threat to the Panama Canal, Arnold and the others launched a competitive airline they called Pan American Airways Inc. that was to operate in the same region as SCADTA and, if all went well, put the German-controlled firm out of business. Washington had just awarded Pan American the Havana mail contract in July of 1927 when the underfunded company, embarrassingly, ran out of money.

Pan American's dilemma was acute: In order to qualify for flying the mail it had to be in the air by October 19. It possessed the critical contract, but no planes, no cash, and moreover, no landing rights in Havana. The men heading the other two interested groups held the missing cards: Hoyt had access to money and Trippe had his letter from President Machado granting him exclusive landing rights in the Cuban capital. Plainly, the three groups had to combine. In negotiating the terms of the merger, Trippe exhibited two traits that were to mark his entire career: calm under stress and a persistence that wore down his adversaries. Offered a minority interest, he smiled and shook his head. He must have control. He would not budge. Finally, the Pan American people caved in. The three companies merged under a new name—Aviation Corporation of the Americas—very similar to the name of Trippe's company. Trippe became president and general manager of Pan American, the operating subsidiary. He was just 28 years old.

Trippe's immediate problems were that two Fokker Trimotors he had ordered had not yet arrived—nor was the Key West landing field ready to receive them. With no planes and with October 19 fast approaching, Trippe's agents desperately began scouring the eastern United States for a seaplane to rent. They heard that a former exhibition pilot named Cyril C. "Cy" Caldwell had just landed in Miami in a single-engined floatplane to be delivered to Haiti. Cash was pressed into Caldwell's hand, seven sacks of mail were crammed into the plane, and on the morning of October 19 he flew them from Key West harbor to Havana. Pan American was in business. A few days later the Trimotors arrived and Key West's rudimentary runway was at last ready for them. The line carried its first passengers on January 16, 1928.

The new firm's emblem was imperial—a globe sprouting eagle's wings—but its visible assets consisted of only two planes, a little ticket office in the arcade of Havana's Biltmore Hotel and another at the Key West airport, and a three-room headquarters office on New York's 42nd Street. So meager were its cash reserves that Trippe accepted stock in lieu of salary and often paid the $60 monthly New York office rent out of his own pocket. His Miami manager listened to his talk of monster seaplanes and transoceanic flights and concluded, as did many others, that Trippe was a crank. But Trippe, in his low-keyed way, had a curiously inspirational power. "He took me out to lunch early in '27," one aeronautical engineer recalled many years later. "After listening to him, I threw up a job that could have been mine for life and joined his hare-brained airline. When I got home I was ashamed to tell my wife."

Others gravitated to the "hare-brained" airline in much the same way. One of the most important of the early arrivals was a little Dutch engineer named André Priester, who soon became known as a wizard of air operations. Trippe relied on him to plan routes, build airports, and above all, hire and train the flying crews whose skill and discipline would become almost legendary in the industry. It was Priester who recruited the most illustrious of all Pan American pilots, a former barnstormer named Edwin C. "Eddie" Musick, who proved so reliable under pressure that the company came to depend on him for almost all of its long-range survey flights.

Perhaps the most striking example of Trippe's shrewd instinct for talent was in his handling of a gangling young Radio Corporation of America engineer named Hugo Leuteritz. Working mostly on his own, Leuteritz had been trying to develop radio navigational equipment for aircraft—essential for long-distance flights over water. While fliers over land could orient themselves by reference to a hilltop beacon, a river or the "iron compass" of a railroad track, at sea there was nothing. Existing radio direction-finding equipment was primitive and too cumbersome for planes. Moreover, in the tropics, where Trippe wanted to fly, atmospheric interference, heard as static in radio receivers, was so intense that pilots could rarely pick up a signal.

Leuteritz thought he could solve these problems, but most airline owners were skeptical and refused to give him money for research. Trippe not only listened but gave Leuteritz $25,000 and permission to install and test his rudimentary equipment on Pan Am planes in Key West. By trial and error, Leuteritz discovered which frequencies would cut through the static, then developed a land-based direction-finding loop large enough to receive signals from planes flying between Key West and Havana. Pilots held down a telegraph-style transmitting key long enough for the loop to be aligned directly on the bearing of the signal coming from the plane. The ground operator then radioed the plane's heading back to the pilot in Morse code. Although Pan Am pilots at first resented being dependent on ground stations, the lightweight navigational system Leuteritz developed eventually enabled Pan Am to fly anywhere in the world. When he had finished his project, Trippe begged him to stay on. "We will fly to Latin America," said Trippe. "We will fly the Atlantic and the Pacific." The magic worked on Leuteritz as it had on others: He joined Pan American.

Trippe performed his magic just as successfully in Washington, for he understood from the beginning that decisions that were made in Washington would ultimately determine whether his airline was to succeed or fail. He was a superb advocate—Senator Kenneth McKellar would later describe him as the most brilliant witness he had ever seen—and he understood whom to cultivate and how to reach them. In the winter of 1928 he was most anxious to confer with Pennsylvania Congressman Clyde Kelly, who had written the domestic airmail act and was now working on its foreign equivalent. Through his former college roommate, son of a multimillionaire Pittsburgh industrialist, Trippe had access to Andrew Mellon, who was not only the wealthiest man in Pittsburgh but also the Secretary of the Treasury. With Mellon interceding for him, Trippe was soon spending long hours with Congressman Kelly helping him to write the bill that would shape the future of overseas commercial flight.

Passed on March 8, 1928, the Kelly Foreign Air Mail Act authorized the appointment of private contractors to carry the mail internationally at a maximum rate of two dollars a mile per pound—higher than the domestic rate because of the higher operational costs involved. The Act also empowered the Postmaster General to decide which bidder could "perform the services required to the best advantage of the government"—a crucial and slippery clause that Trippe would later exploit with consummate skill.

A few weeks after the Act was passed, bids were invited on two new overseas routes—one heading east from Cuba via Puerto Rico and the Leeward and Windward Islands to Trinidad, and the other from Cuba westward to Yucatan and down through Central America to Panama. When Pan American was awarded both contracts at the maximum rate, rumors began circulating that just a few days before bids were invited Postmaster General Harry New had consulted with Trippe about the best routes to Latin America. Even before that, Trippe's agents had been in cities along the future air routes seeking exclusive landing rights for Pan American. To critics, this looked like collusion between Pan

Vacationers board a Fokker Trimotor in Key West, Florida, for Pan American Airways' first passenger flight to Havana, Cuba, in 1928. The $50 one-way fare was steep for the time, yet more than 1,100 tickets were sold the first year.

American and the government—a charge that would be brought against Trippe repeatedly throughout his career.

In fact, Washington's early and continuing sympathy for Pan American was almost inevitable, for no other owners knew quite as much as Juan Trippe did about the problems of overseas flight. In those early years, he would sometimes disappear from his New York office for weeks on end to pilot a little single-engined Fairchild on solo survey flights that he talked about to nobody. He was exploring approaches to South America via three possible trunk lines: two of them along the Post Office routes eventually announced and a third from Texas through Mexico to connect with the Panama route. Beyond these, he envisioned lines stretching down both coasts of the South American continent and coming together at Buenos Aires.

To realize his ambitious schemes, which involved a great deal of flying over water, Trippe needed something other than the land-based Fokkers he had been using up to then: He turned to Russian émigré designer-manufacturer Igor Sikorsky and ordered a number of twin-engined planes with alternative landplane and seaplane gear.

At the same time, Trippe set to work getting control over the routes. The quickest procedure, he found, often was to swallow whatever airlines existed, taking over their contractual arrangements with local governments. This he did on the Cuba-Puerto Rico run, absorbing an outfit called West Indian Aerial Express. Founded in 1927 by a former air racer, the line had been counting heavily on winning the Cuba-Puerto Rico airmail contract—West Indian's by right, its managers felt, because it was the only airline already flying the route. What they did not realize until too late, the line's pilot-owner recalled with chagrin some years later, was that "while we had been developing an air line in the West Indies our competitors had been busy on the much more important job of developing a lobby in Washington." When Pan Am won the government contract, Trippe promptly bought out West Indian and took over both its route and the landing concessions it had obtained.

Working in his favor was the unwritten precept of the chosen instrument that, with Trippe's encouragement, had taken strong hold in Washington. Inside the United States, the theory went, the country would benefit from rivalry between airlines, but overseas competition was harmful: Only a single, favored airline, enjoying the full support of the government, could compete against state-backed foreign lines such as Germany's Luft Hansa, France's Aéropostale and Britain's Imperial Airways. Trippe was to use the argument for many years with overwhelming success. And it so permeated United States political thinking that in 1941 a Congressional committee would state frankly that "distasteful as monopoly may be under ordinary conditions, the fact remains that our foreign air operation is a monopoly, instituted and encouraged by the government."

The shape of the monopoly began to become clear in 1929, when Pan Am was awarded its third overseas mail contract, for the route south

On this 1929 Pan Am baggage sticker, a stylish couple sets off for a Caribbean island holiday. During the Prohibition era in the United States, many wealthy and thirsty Americans were attracted to the free-wheeling island resorts shown on the map.

from Texas through Mexico. A year earlier, Trippe had laid the groundwork by gobbling up an American-run Mexican airline known as Compañía Mexicana de Aviación *(pages 66-67)*. Although his bid was higher than those of six competitors, he got the contract anyway, because he was the only one who owned a Mexican airline—and foreign lines, by Mexican law, were not allowed to fly mail over the country.

In winning the contracts for these initial southern mail routes, Trippe secured an assured $50 million in mail revenues for Pan American over the next 10 years. Company stock soared, ensuring that Trippe would become a multimillionaire. In the first flush of success he married Elizabeth Stettinius, daughter of a J. P. Morgan partner and sister of a college friend, Edward Stettinius, who was later to be Chairman of the Board of Directors of U.S. Steel Corporation and United States Secretary of State.

Another man who became rich with Pan American was the company's technical adviser, Charles A. Lindbergh. Trippe and Lindbergh met in February of 1928, some eight months after the Lone Eagle's solo flight from New York to Paris. Trippe asked the new hero to serve as consultant to Pan American, a post that Lindbergh formally accepted in 1929, agreeing to take part of his compensation in stock options. Although Lindbergh did not work exclusively for Trippe, his advice helped shape Pan American policy for three decades to come.

Lindbergh offered advice on nothing he had not observed himself. Assigned by Trippe early in 1929 to simultaneously survey and inaugurate the 2,000-mile Cuba-Panama airmail route, Lindbergh refused to be distracted by the crowds that mobbed him at every stop. Flying over Central American mountain ranges, deserts and jungles that were virtually inaccessible to railroads, he searched for locations along the route where airfields could be built—for landplanes would obviously be the best to use here—and where navigational equipment could be installed. From Cristobal he sent Trippe a long telegram describing what he had seen. On Lindbergh's heels, and those of other aerial surveyors, Pan American construction crews moved in by ship and canoe, by burro and on foot, hacking their way through miles of dense jungle toward the white splotches on the ground where survey pilots had dropped bags of flour to indicate airfield sites. The crews took six months to lay a network of landing fields and navigational posts across the 800 miles of malarial jungle and swamp lying between Panama and British Honduras.

Long before they were finished, Juan Trippe was looking even farther south. Moving fast to secure the continent's west coast, he took over a small crop-dusting concern in Peru—it had been operated by the people who later founded Delta Airlines in the United States—and renamed it Peruvian Airways. Still farther south, he set up a company in Santiago and called it Chilean Airways. And for $1.1 million he bought a controlling interest in the German-run Colombian airline SCADTA—although for political reasons the sale was kept secret and Germans continued to operate the line.

Juan Trippe (right) and Charles Lindbergh confer on the runway after landing in Panama on the return leg of the first United States mail flight to South America in 1929. Lindbergh's fame sparked interest wherever they went, while Trippe followed through with hardheaded business deals.

The most monumental barrier to his ambition was the massive American trading conglomerate W. R. Grace and Company, which, according to one of Trippe's field agents, "owned practically everything on the west coast" of South America. Any airline flying in their territory, Grace's owners felt, should belong to them. On the other hand, Grace's hope of establishing its own air link to the United States was frustrated by Pan Am's control of Panama and the route north. Mutually blocked, the two corporations decided to combine forces in a jointly owned company called Pan American-Grace Airways, or Panagra—although the corporate marriage was a severe blow to Trippe's pride. Within two weeks of its founding, Panagra won a whopping new airmail contract on a route running 4,500 miles south from Panama to Chile and then across the Andes to Buenos Aires and Montevideo.

Soon after that, in an exuberant mood, Trippe and his wife accompanied Lindbergh and his bride of four months on an inaugural flight extending the Cuba-Puerto Rico route south beyond Trinidad to Dutch

A challenger's fall

Ambitious 33-year-old World War I ace Ralph O'Neill thought he was bringing a dream to life when, in 1929, he raised five million dollars and founded the New York, Rio, and Buenos Aires airline, or NYRBA. But the grandiose name was premature. O'Neill mapped a 7,800-mile route between New York and Argentina, but by 1930 he had established only two short runs out of Buenos Aires.

In February, trying to prove his line worthy of a United States mail contract, he lost three planes to crashes and one to a legal dispute during a futile six-day attempt to get a cargo of Argentine mail to New York. Finally, using Consolidated Commodore flying boats, he established regular Florida-to-Argentina passenger service. But the line lost money, and in September 1930 his backers sold out to Pan American, which promptly got a mail contract and began making a healthy profit on NYRBA's routes.

RALPH O'NEILL, PRESIDENT OF NYRBA

A Commodore "flying yacht" wings over Rio in a NYRBA poster.

Guiana. (Coincidentally, both wives had J. P. Morgan connections: Like the elder Stettinius, Anne Lindbergh's father, Dwight Morrow, had been a Morgan partner.) Young and abundantly successful, both couples remembered the flight long afterward as a kind of exotic confirmation of a future in which everything suddenly seemed possible.

With Lindbergh at the controls of the latest Sikorsky amphibian, they flew 9,000 miles over tropical seas, virgin jungles and occasional beaches pink with flamingos. At Paramaribo in Dutch Guiana, local women took off their great turban headdresses and spread them on the dock for the visitors to walk on as they came ashore. As the Lindberghs and the Trippes made their royal way through Venezuela and Colombia and back up through Central America, Anne Lindbergh observed Trippe closely. She described him later as "a great big bumbling bear of a man" who seemed younger than the 30 years of age he then was and "gave a sense of great good nature." What impressed her most, though, was an energy that seemed never to flag: While the rest of the party slept late after the banquets that greeted them at virtually every stop, Trippe rose early each morning to consult with government and postal authorities about the kinds of problems his airline might expect to meet in these strange new skies.

Pan American had locked up the west coast of South America. It needed only the east-coast link between Buenos Aires and Dutch Guiana to complete a circuit of the continent. That stretch was crucial, for it covered the biggest cities. It also seemed inaccessible: For the first time another American, fully as ambitious as Trippe, had arrived in a prospective area before him, and had done so with elaborate plans, solid Wall Street financing and the very latest aircraft. Ralph O'Neill was an aggressive, strong-willed flyer who had won three Distinguished Service Crosses in World War I. In 1926 he conceived the idea of an airline running a full 7,800 miles from New York all the way down to Buenos Aires via the West Indies and South America's populous east coast. Equipped with twin-engined Consolidated Commodore flying boats, the New York, Rio, and Buenos Aires Line—known in the industry as NYRBA *(page 152)*—established regular flights between Buenos Aires and Miami and demonstrated its ability to carry Argentine mail to the United States mainland in six days.

In 1930, O'Neill had a functioning airline, but he was in trouble. His chief financial backer, James Rand, Chairman of the Board of Remington Rand, the office equipment company, had lost millions in the stock-market crash, and NYRBA itself was losing money—partly because it had no permit to fly United States mail south. In this crisis, O'Neill made an error that other rivals of Trippe had made in the past: He neglected to lobby in Washington. Soon it became apparent that Postmaster General Walter Brown favored Pan American and had no intention of inviting competitive bidding for airmail service on South America's east coast. "Competitive bidding in the airmail business," he said with a candor rare in public servants, "is more or less of a myth."

He advised NYRBA to sell out to Pan Am, and eventually the company was forced to do so. In victory, Juan Trippe drove a hard bargain. "If the argument had run a week longer," said James Rand ruefully, "I would have given Trippe our company for nothing." As it was, Pan Am got the airline for a price that gave NYRBA investors only 40 cents for each dollar they had put in. Immediately thereafter Pan Am got the Dutch Guiana-Buenos Aires airmail route as well. Looking back at the battle, Trippe wrote off NYRBA in a typically dry—and brutally accurate—comment. "They were nice young men who thought they would like to run an international air line," he said. "But they didn't really know what it was all about."

Whether Trippe was a nice young man nobody was sure, but clearly he knew what running an international airline was all about. In just three years he had transformed an airline that flew one 90-mile route into a company that flew 20,308 miles in 20 countries. At the age of 31, he was the head of the biggest airline in the world, in terms of route miles.

To critics, Pan American looked too big—a kind of state within a state that was intent on extending its influence over the economic and political life of the countries its service reached. Although the criticism was simplistic—Pan American for the most part went to great lengths to avoid any involvement in local politics—the company's sheer economic weight obviously affected those countries. Its presence encouraged United States investment in Central and South America and influenced the socioeconomic development of the entire continent, if only because it linked scattered population centers that formerly had been isolated by mountain and jungle. And inevitably the company became involved, willingly or otherwise, in the turbulent life of the region. Airline personnel not only got caught in the cross fire of revolution—one flying boat took off near Montenegro, Brazil, with riflemen aiming at it—but also flew scores of humanitarian missions to deliver medicine and evacuate victims in earthquake and hurricane disasters. Throughout Latin America, the Pan American planes became the most visible symbol of the Good Neighbor Policy that was insistently proclaimed by Washington during the 1930s.

To the uninformed, the Pan American crews could easily be mistaken for United States military personnel: Uniforms were dark blue, in the naval tradition, while the pilot was called captain and his copilot first officer. Speed was figured in knots, and time was sounded in bells.

At this early high point of his career, Trippe remained personally a mystery. "Juan is essentially a lonely man," said one of his oldest friends. "He doesn't explain himself easily." Indeed, he explained himself so reluctantly that his associates rarely knew what he was about to do. At staff meetings it was his practice to pull a few scribbled notes from his pocket and without warning announce the launching of a new project—whether it was to purchase a different aircraft or to extend operations across a new sea. Often the notes disappeared directly into a wastebasket at his feet, leaving no official record behind. To a remarkable degree, as one associate remarked, "he carried Pan American in his mind."

In his restless, visionary way, he was turning his attention now to other ocean routes. He was sure it would soon be possible for commercial aircraft to span the Atlantic—probably via Bermuda and the Azores to Lisbon. He opened negotiations with the British and French to arrange joint development of a transatlantic route. But the Europeans demanded reciprocal rights for their airlines—rights an isolationist United States government was reluctant to grant. Britain further stipulated that no service with the United States could be inaugurated until both parties were ready, and Britain was not ready. So Trippe put aside his Atlantic plans for the moment and looked to the Pacific instead.

First he needed an amphibious plane larger than any that then existed. He turned again to Igor Sikorsky, who responded brilliantly with the S-40, the first four-engined flying boat ever built in America. These magnificent planes held 50 passengers in walnut-paneled comfort and, when fully loaded, had a range of close to 1,000 miles. Trippe decreed that they would be called clippers in sentimental tribute to the swift ships his seafaring ancestors had known in glorious times long past.

Even as the first clipper was being flown by Lindbergh from Miami to Colombia, Sikorsky was pondering the plane's successor. At one point on that epochal inaugural flight, Lindbergh turned over the controls to the copilot and, joining Sikorsky in the cabin, sketched on the back of a dinner menu the cleaner, more powerful aircraft he would like to see next. Some of Lindbergh's ideas were duly incorporated in the Sikorsky S-42, which had a range nearly three times that of the original clipper. Meanwhile, Trippe had also asked Glenn Martin to design a plane capable of transoceanic flight.

In 1933, Pan American had a sizable portion of its capital invested in the construction of clippers that as yet had no place to go: Negotiations for a transatlantic route had come to nothing, and a Pacific air track had not yet been developed. Furthermore, there was no way for an aircraft to navigate accurately more than 600 miles from land—the outer limit of Hugo Leuteritz's direction finders. By the summer of 1935, Leuteritz had managed to develop a direction-finding system with a theoretical range of 2,400 miles—just enough to track the clippers. But he was not at all sure that the system would actually work; later, when he looked back on the project, he was amazed at Trippe's cool daring in gambling millions of dollars and Pan American's future on a navigation system— and on air routes—that did not yet exist.

So secretive was Trippe that none of his associates knew for certain where he planned to use the new clippers until, at a board meeting in December 1934, he remarked quietly, "We are getting ready to fly the Pacific." Trippe had at first thought that transpacific flight should be routed by way of Alaska, and in 1931 Lindergh, in company with his wife, surveyed a great circle route via Point Barrow, Alaska, and Japan to China. Lindbergh reported that a northern path was indeed feasible.

Laying Pan Am's Pacific steppingstones

When Pan American Airways decided to extend its air routes to the Orient in 1935 it undertook a project that was later called the "most spectacular move in the history of airline operations"—building or improving four remote bases in the Pacific to guide, refuel and supply the clipper flying boats along their 8,000-mile course to Asia.

In March the steamer *North Haven* sailed from San Francisco with some 120 workers and a hold filled with construction equipment and meticulously planned packages of supplies—more than 100,000 items in all. At Midway atoll, workers took 10 days to unload equipment, including a 10-ton tractor, and ferry it ashore in 10-foot waves. Once the Midway radio station was operating and construction of the crews' quarters and dock were under way, the *North Haven* proceeded to the even more desolate Wake Island.

There, the men had to improvise a 200-yard railroad to haul their materials across an adjacent islet before construction could begin. After the remaining crews and supplies were off-loaded at Guam and Manila to upgrade United States Navy facilities for Pan American's use, the *North Haven* returned to San Francisco in July.

But her mission was not yet completed. Shortly after regular mail flights began in December, the *North Haven* was back in the Pacific, carrying an expedition to build hotels for the passengers who would start flying the route in 1936.

A dynamite blast clears coral heads from the lagoon at Wake Island. It took five months and five tons of dynamite to clear a safe landing area for the clippers.

Workmen roll gasoline drums ferried ashore from the North Haven (background) across a hastily built dock on Wake atoll.

Gooney birds congregate near the finished crew quarters at the Pan Am clipper base on Midway atoll. The rustic village offered private rooms, hot and cold running water, a library and frequent movies.

Workmen inch a crated generator up a hill to the site of the Pan Am radio station in the Philippines. The station was part of the communications and navigation system developed for the Pacific route by the line's communications engineer, Hugo Leuteritz.

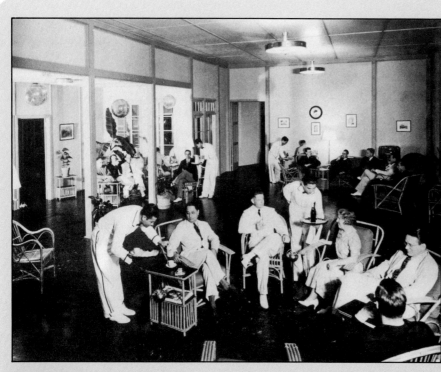

Clipper passengers on the five-day flight from San Francisco to Manila enjoy a stopover on Wake Island in the lounge of a hotel that Pan American built expressly for their use. Hotels were also constructed on Midway atoll and Guam.

Grown on soil shipped to barren Midway from Guam, a lawn at the airline's hotel provides a promenade for the ubiquitous gooney birds.

Shortly thereafter, Trippe acquired a majority interest in an airline operating in China called the China National Aviation Corporation. Then the U.S. State Department waved him off the route: Diplomatic relations with the Soviet Union, which stood astride the track, were deteriorating and those with Japan were similarly poor.

The other way to go was straight across the open ocean, hopping from island to island all the way to the Asian mainland. The difficulties were awesome. The 2,400 miles that lay between California and Hawaii constituted the longest overwater jump in the world: Many fliers had lost their lives attempting it, and Trippe did not even know if the new planes he had ordered were capable of spanning it. Midway, the next step, had a lagoon that would be suitable for landing, but after that came Wake Island—a treeless, uninhabited atoll that had been so rarely visited that nobody could tell the Pan American planners whether it offered shelter for a flying boat or not. All Trippe and his associates knew for certain was that there would be no diplomatic problems—for all the prospective landing sites, which included Guam and the Philippines, were under United States control.

The first Sikorsky S-42, test-flown by Lindbergh, handled superlatively, but its range was only about 2,540 miles—not enough to ensure safe arrival in Hawaii. The plane was put into service in the Caribbean, and Trippe had the range of a second S-42 stretched by 500 miles by the addition of extra fuel tanks so that it could begin long-range survey flights over the Pacific routes that would be flown by the larger, more powerful Martins.

Certain now that he would have equipment capable of flying the Pacific, Trippe next approached Washington for an airmail contract. In his letter to Postmaster General James Farley, he took the kind of strongly patriotic line that had prompted one State Department official to remark dryly: "Trippe always puts America first, but sometimes it is hard to tell whether he is being pro-American or pro-Pan American." In this case, he reminded Farley that unspecified foreign airlines were making "aggressive" approaches to the other side of the Pacific. In return, he got only the assurance that the Post Office Department was interested in Pan American's plans.

With or without a contract, Trippe was determined to go ahead: On March 27, 1935, he dispatched an expedition to build bases on Midway, Wake and Guam. Crammed into the chartered freighter *North Haven* as it sailed from San Francisco were all the supplies that would be needed to construct and operate the island airports. For four months construction crews labored under the Pacific sun—clearing away the jungle growth, erecting radio masts and buildings, and dynamiting channels through the outcroppings of the coral reefs so the flying boats could land *(pages 156-158)*.

In the meantime, Eddie Musick had brought the modified S-42 from Miami by way of Cuba, Veracruz and Acapulco to the Pacific and up the coast to San Francisco. An exhaustive round of tests fol-

With Eddie Musick at the controls (inset), a clipper soars over the unfinished Golden Gate Bridge on Pan Am's first airmail flight to Manila in 1935.

lowed as a preliminary to ocean flying. "The only way to do it was to do it," John Leslie, the Pan Am engineer in charge of testing, recalled many years later. "We pushed the state of the art as far as space engineers did when they sent men to the moon. We were at the extreme limit, in fact a little beyond."

Musick and his crew practiced radio-beam flying, blind approaches and even totally blind landings. On April 16, 1935, he took off for Honolulu. Guided by radio signals sent out by ships positioned along the route, he flew through the darkness and in the morning circled over Pearl Harbor and landed.

Four days later came the return trip—and near-disaster. Immediately after takeoff the S-42 encountered stiff head winds. Hour after hour it inched eastward with all four engines running at the lowest possible speed to preserve fuel. In its longest previous test flight, it had remained aloft for just over 17 hours. Now it had been in the air for 18 hours, and it still had 500 miles to go. When the aerial navigator calculated the plane's ground speed at only 96 miles per hour, Eddie Musick and his copilot fell silent and began peering intently through the windshield for the first shadow of land. Finally, five hours overdue, the plane broke out of the overcast, and Musick saw the San Francisco hills ahead. Soon the airport was in sight. Unwilling to spend any fuel circling for a better landing approach, he came straight in. When the plane was down and the engines had been cut, the engineer put a stick into the fuel tanks and found them barely wet.

The first Martin M-130 clipper was delivered in October 1935. One third bigger than the S-42, it was both an engineering and an esthetic triumph. Packed with safety features that had been demanded by Priester—dual hydraulic and electrical systems, multiple bulkheads—it cruised at 150 miles per hour and had a range of 3,200 miles fully loaded. Although it was the largest flying boat in scheduled service, it managed to convey a feeling of grace and style. The interior was like that of an elegant small hotel and it boasted a well-equipped galley in which an entire meal could be prepared aloft.

Trippe by now had secured the transpacific mail contract by his familiar tactic of buying out the potential competition—in this case, two newly formed Hawaiian airlines, Inter-Island Airways and South Seas Commercial—that had their eyes on the China trade. Shortly thereafter, the first Clipper landed at Wake Island—with difficulty, for the lagoon was not yet free of coral obstructions. Nevertheless, Trippe felt he could wait no longer to inaugurate mail service. On November 22, 1935, Farley made his speech, rockets burst, whistles shrilled, and the China Clipper lifted off from San Francisco Bay and headed for Hawaii. That first flight—and all succeeding flights for nearly a year—carried mail only, for the hotels that were to accommodate passengers on Midway, Wake and Guam were not yet completed.

At the outset, the China Clipper was misnamed. Pan American had not yet been granted landing rights in China; its western Pacific terminus was Manila. On the other hand, Pan Am still controlled the China National Aviation Corporation and so could fly passengers on the mainland. Trippe requested permission to land in the British crown colony of Hong Kong, where transpacific passengers would be able to transfer to CNAC planes. At first the British balked: Imperial Airways wanted to reserve Hong Kong landing rights exclusively for its own planes. Trippe coolly negotiated with the Portuguese for landing rights in nearby Macao, announced that he would soon begin operations, and sat back to wait. In no time British and Chinese businessmen in Hong Kong were petitioning London to grant Pan American permission to land. Britain gave in.

Now able to provide service all the way to the Chinese mainland—and with the island hotels completed—Pan American in October 1936 began transporting passengers as well as mail across the Pacific. The nine adventurous souls who signed up for that first flight paid a princely price—$1,438.20 round trip to Manila—but the accommodations and services were correspondingly regal. The *Clipper's* central lounge, which was wider than a Pullman club car, was fitted with broad armchairs, and its meal service included china and silverware. At the palm-girt mid-ocean hotels, passengers sipped iced tea on the broad verandas and were served in the dining rooms by islanders dressed in immaculate white uniforms.

Trippe now saw no reason not to set up a branch line to Australia and New Zealand. Once again the British tried to block the way: Already flying to Australia, they did not wish to allow Pan American access unless the United States permitted them to serve Hawaii—which it would not do. Australia bowed to British pressure and refused Trippe landing rights. He then began a campaign in New Zealand stressing the economic benefits the country could expect if it became the terminus of the principal South Pacific air route. His arguments were persuasive: New Zealand officials enthusiastically accepted Trippe's offer—and were startled to learn that Pan Am's inaugural flight would arrive only six days later. For Trippe once again had been thinking ahead and had scouted intervening landing sites at Kingman Reef, a Wake-like atoll south of Hawaii, and at Pago Pago in American Samoa. Kingman Reef was made usable by the simple expedient of stationing a small tanker in its lagoon to refuel clippers; Pago Pago was a bona fide settlement with a harbor where planes could land, although with difficulty, and with adequate fuel. Eddie Musick inaugurated the service to Auckland in March 1937.

Only nine months later, a tragedy on the New Zealand route called the whole service into question. Musick was some 75 miles off Pago Pago on another survey flight when his plane exploded—presumably because of a fuel leak—and all seven aboard were killed. Six months after that, a clipper from San Francisco crashed between Guam and Manila, killing six passengers and a crew of nine. The two disasters reduced Pan American's Pacific fleet to two Martin flying boats, forcing

Surrounded by welcoming boats, Pan Am's China Clipper lies moored in Manila Bay after its island-hopping six-day flight from San Francisco.

the company to cut its schedule by 60 per cent. In any case, after the two incidents passenger business declined sharply.

With losses on the route now nearing $100,000 a month, and with public confidence in Pan American badly shaken, Trippe was criticized heavily from both outside and inside the company. The prevailing mood was summed up by pioneer aircraft builder Grover Loening, who had resigned from Pan Am's board in protest over the decision to fly to Hawaii. "This accident," said Loening of the *Hawaii Clipper* crash, "brings into focus the monopolistic aims of this one company in a tragic blunder of overexpansion, underpreparation and overworking of its personnel." After the Musick crash the U.S. Department of Commerce withdrew its authorization of Pago Pago as a landing site, and New Zealand flights were suspended while a new route was devised.

Characteristically, Trippe reacted to this shift in Pan Am's fortunes by pushing even harder. His attention turned once again to the Atlantic. In 1935, the U.S. State Department had taken over Atlantic route negotiations on behalf of all United States airlines. In fact, the State Department had come to an agreement with England that the two countries would share in a reciprocal United States-England air service that would operate for a minimum of 15 years. The problem was that Britain still insisted on holding up service until everyone was ready—and as yet the British had no planes that were capable of flying the Atlantic. Meanwhile, adopting the technique they had started using on the South Atlantic route in 1933 *(page 42),* the Germans had begun crossing the North Atlantic by catapulting planes from two strategically placed supply ships—one stationed in Long Island Sound and the other positioned near the Azores for mid-Atlantic refueling.

Although he did not yet have an Atlantic route, Trippe was close to having a plane to fly it: the whale-shaped Boeing B-314. He had ordered the new aircraft from Boeing in 1936 after Sikorsky and Martin had both bowed out because the hardheaded Trippe refused to share development costs for a new design. (To Glenn Martin's complaint that Trippe had ruined him and betrayed an old business relationship in turning to Boeing, Trippe replied bluntly: "We're businessmen; we can't have friends.")

Boeing developed the new plane from plans for a four-engined bomber that its designers had drawn up for the Army. "We've got this bomber design," said Boeing engineer Wellwood Beall. "Take the wing and put a hull under it."

The B-314 *(pages 168-169)* was the finest flying boat ever produced and the largest commercial plane to fly until the arrival of the jumbo jets 30 years later. Double-decked, it could seat 74 passengers or sleep 40 in berths. Its top speed was 193 miles per hour and its range was 3,500 miles. Mechanics could service any of its four engines during flight from inside the monster wing.

On February 22, 1939, the B-314 replaced the Martin M-130 on the northern Pacific route; on July 12, 1940, it reopened the southern

DOMAIN OF PHOEBUS APOLLO

Ruler of the Sun and Heavens

INTERNATIONAL DATE LINE

Pacific Ocean

SAN FRANCISCO

MIDWAY

HONOLULU

HONGKONG MACAO MANILA

WAKE

GUAM

Trans-Pacific Route
PAN AMERICAN
AIRWAYS SYSTEM

Know All Peoples

That *H.G.Gulbransen*, once earthbound and time-laden, is now declared a subject of the Realm of the Sun and of the Heavens, with the freedom of our Sacred Eagle..... That with the speed of Our Flaming Chariot this subject did fly the Pacific skies over the International Date Line, which mortals designed to mark off in the limit of days Our Eternal Course through the skies..... That by so crossing this divider of days between the earth isles of Midway and Wake, the Today of mortals at once becomes Tomorrow and all is confusion..... That this subject is commanded to hold ever close this Celestial Decree so that in the final accounting of earthly days, the balance will stand true..... Done in the Realm of the Sun and of the Heavens by the order of Phoebus Apollo, Rex, Son of Zeus and Leto.

Aboard *China Clipper* *9.44 a.m.* *November 29-30, 1936* *John H. Tiller* Captain.

Time of Crossing   Emissary Plenipotentiary

A "Celestial Decree," given to clipper passengers crossing the international date line in the 1930s, bears a florid inscription purportedly written by Apollo, the sun god of ancient Greece, and a map identifying the crossing point as a spot "between the earth isles of Midway and Wake."

Pacific route, flying to New Zealand via Canton Island and New Caledonia. The plane was also Trippe's answer to the diplomatic logjam over Atlantic service, for it would be able to outflank the British, jumping over Bermuda to reach the Azores in one hop and then flying on to Lisbon and Marseilles. By early 1939 the British, now preoccupied with the threat of war, gave up and permitted Pan Am entry into England. Trippe prepared for the inaugural flight.

At that moment, when he seemed to be at his apogee, Trippe was deposed by his board of directors. Pan Am was in financial trouble: The Pacific division was in the red, and the Atlantic operations would take a long time to earn back their heavy development costs. This might have been acceptable if Trippe had confided in the board, but he was as secretive as ever. Ironically, the appointed leader of the opposition was one of Trippe's earliest backers, Cornelius Vanderbilt Whitney, who had been with him since Eastern Air Transport days. Pan Am's largest single stockholder, Sonny Whitney had become alarmed by the increasingly heavy debts the company was incurring to finance the global expansion. At a board meeting on March 14, 1939, Whitney—already nominally chairman of the board—was elected chief executive officer of the company. Trippe remained as president, but it was an empty title, for he was to report to Whitney.

An odd period in executive relationships ensued. Whitney moved into Trippe's corner office. From a smaller office to which he had been banished, Trippe noted who came to see Whitney and how often. When Whitney held staff meetings, Trippe would attend politely but say nothing. When the first of the Boeing flying boats, christened the *Yankee Clipper,* took off from New York in June on its long-heralded first transatlantic passenger flight, Trippe was not present, having gone to England. Months passed, and the company seemed to stagnate. Leadership was so weak that though war was raging in Europe the company had not even begun to formulate a plan for operating under wartime conditions. At length the inevitable decision was made: No one else could run Pan American, if only because no one else knew what was in Juan Trippe's head. In January 1940, he was restored to full power.

The repercussions of those troubled 10 months were felt long afterward—for Trippe was a man who did not forget. Executives who had accepted Whitney too enthusiastically suddenly found that they could no longer get in to see Trippe in person. Among those who fell from his favor were Charles Lindbergh and Hugo Leuteritz, both of whom eventually left the company (Lindbergh later returned).

Nor were Pan American's troubles with the coveted Atlantic run entirely over. In the spring of 1939, the newly formed American Export Airlines, a subsidiary of the steamship company of similar name, applied to the Civil Aeronautics Board for authority to fly to Europe. Alarmed at this prospect of competition, Trippe now launched an attack that led American Export to label Pan Am as one of the smoothest and most powerful lobbying organizations in the country.

So skillfully did Pan American's lawyers maneuver that, even though the Post Office, State, Navy and War Departments favored a second airline over the Atlantic, American Export was denied the necessary airmail appropriations by vote of the House Appropriations Committee—and hence was effectively barred from the Atlantic until its planes were pressed into emergency wartime service in 1942. At the same time, Pan American set up a puppet airline in Guatemala that successfully scuttled a local airline that American Export was planning to buy.

Carrying mainly military personnel and high-priority civilian travelers, Pan American Airways operated a restricted passenger service over both the Atlantic and the Pacific throughout World War II. When the War ended, Juan Trippe and the company he had created found themselves in a different world. The great flying boats were superseded by

Puffing thoughtfully on his pipe, Juan Trippe surveys his empire in this 1941 publicity shot. Such pictures encouraged tales that Trippe planned Pan Am's routes simply by stretching bits of string around his office globe; in fact, he depended on thorough surveys by teams of experts.

A Pan American Airways B-314 flying boat lifts off from San Francisco Bay for a transpacific flight to Hong Kong in 1941. After the United States entered the War later that year, the luxurious clippers became military transports, ferrying VIPs and high-priority cargo to every theater of battle.

four-engined landplanes, and modern airstrips were available every-where. But from Trippe's point of view, the most important change was that the principle of exclusivity had disappeared. Although he would remain at the head of Pan American until 1968—becoming the last of commercial aviation's pioneering leaders to go—Trippe never again saw his enormously successful airline enjoy the role of a chosen in-strument. Competition was now deemed better for the industry and for the public as well.

Indeed, World War II changed the entire complexion of commercial aviation. In the postwar world, with its rapidly decreasing air fares, flying would no longer be a mode of transport largely reserved for the well to do. Nor would it be largely in the hands of the daring entrepreneurs whose visionary spirit Juan Trippe so exemplified. Some of the great venturous airline enterprises these men launched survived, some merged, some ceased to exist. But they left as a permanent legacy a shrunken and more cohesive globe: Peoples once separated by weeks or months of arduous travel had become virtual neighbors. Old con-cepts of distance and time had forever disappeared.

With the globe encircled by a network of air routes, the frontier was no longer geographical: From now on, the airlines of the world would turn their attention to carrying a mass rather than an elite public—at lower and lower fares and greater and greater speeds. ～

Anatomy of Pan Am's flying hotel

From the outside, the Boeing B-314, the largest airplane of its day, had the appearance of a giant blue whale with rigid wings on its back. Yet the interior of this airborne colossus, used by Pan American for both its Atlantic and Pacific clipper services, was fitted out like a suite at the Ritz.

Built to carry 74 passengers and a crew of eight, the 314 was equipped with sleeping berths for 40, separate dressing rooms for men and women and a well-stocked bar amidships. It also had a lounge that doubled as a

dining room, and a deluxe cabin in the tail section that converted into a bridal suite. The 106-foot-long fuselage was divided into two levels connected by a spiral staircase. Passengers sat below in groups of 10 in soundproof compartments while the crew inhabited the upper level, where baggage and freight were stowed. The plane was constructed of aluminum alloy on a central frame of steel. A walkway inside each wing allowed flight engineers to reach all four engines in case in-flight repairs were needed.

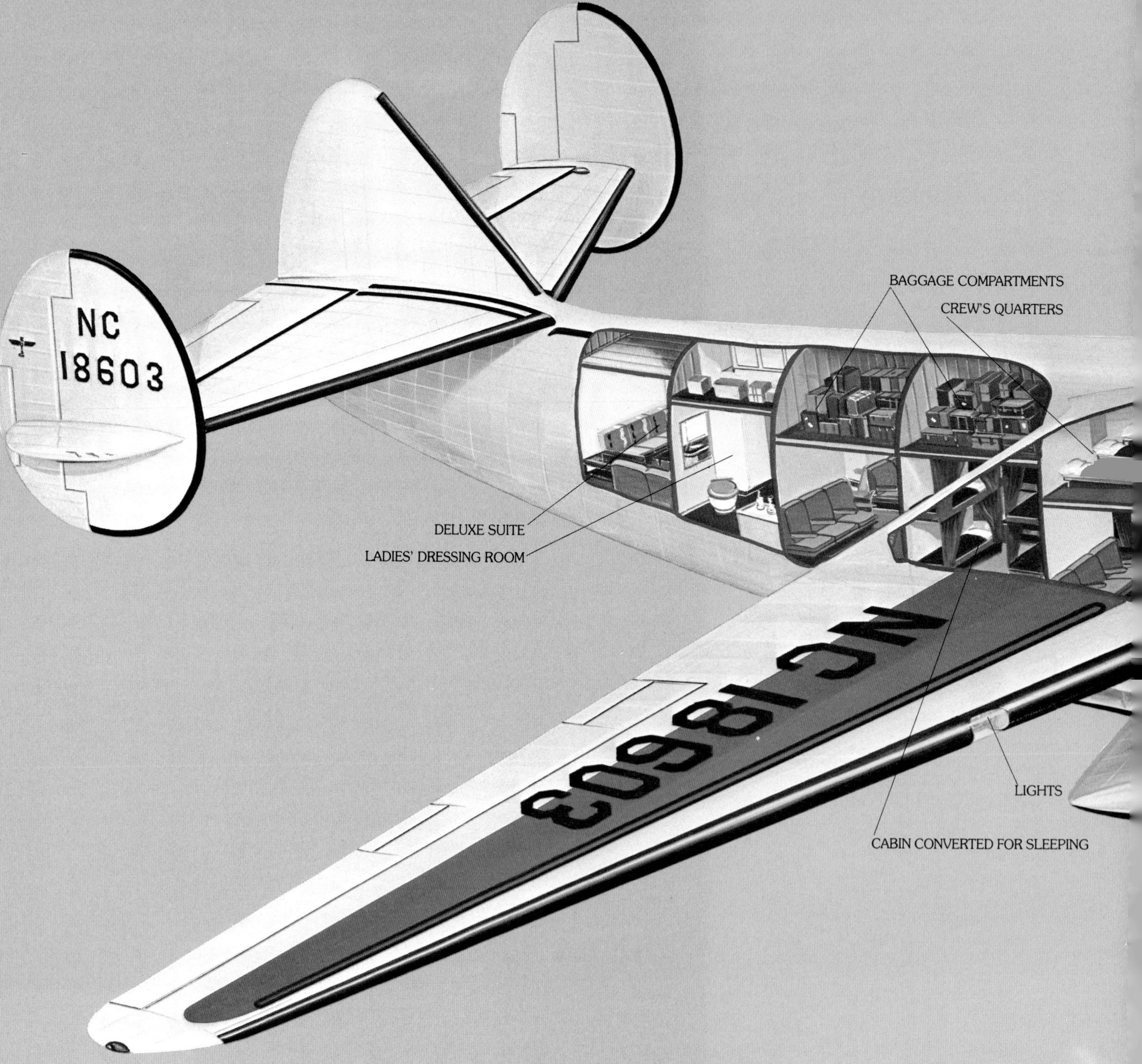

NC
18603

BAGGAGE COMPARTMENTS

CREW'S QUARTERS

DELUXE SUITE

LADIES' DRESSING ROOM

NC18603

LIGHTS

CABIN CONVERTED FOR SLEEPING

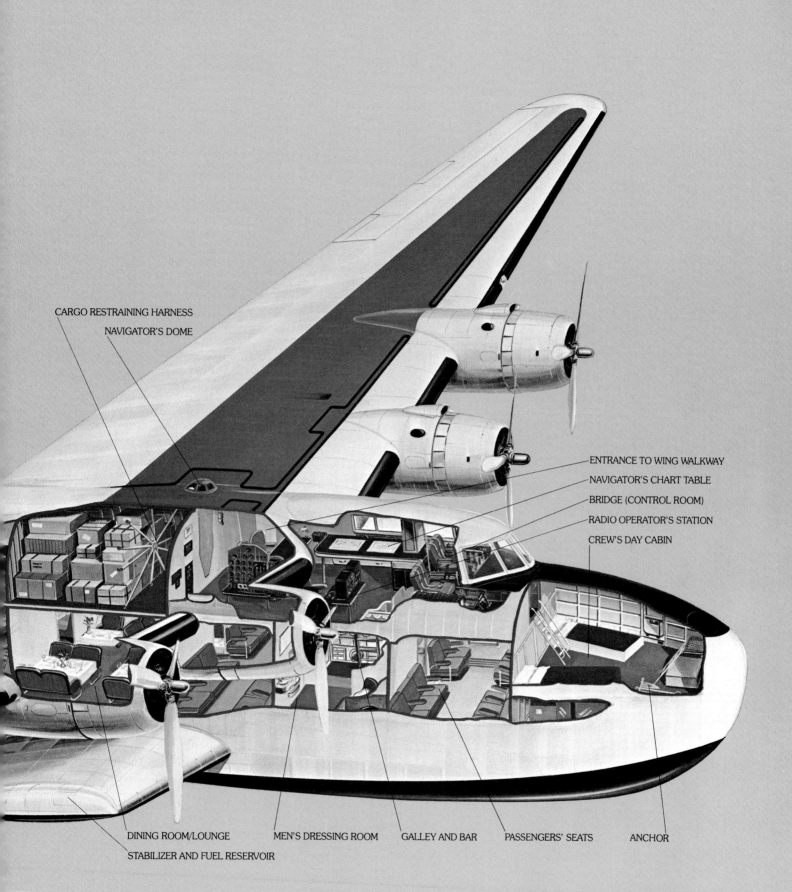

CARGO RESTRAINING HARNESS

NAVIGATOR'S DOME

ENTRANCE TO WING WALKWAY

NAVIGATOR'S CHART TABLE

BRIDGE (CONTROL ROOM)

RADIO OPERATOR'S STATION

CREW'S DAY CABIN

DINING ROOM/LOUNGE

MEN'S DRESSING ROOM

GALLEY AND BAR

PASSENGERS' SEATS

ANCHOR

STABILIZER AND FUEL RESERVOIR

Propelled by four 1,500-hp Wright Double Cyclone engines whose combined power was equal to that of two locomotives, the 314 could cruise for 3,500 miles at a speed of 175 mph without refueling. It made the London-to-New York flight in 23 hours.

The genealogies of the airlines

The charts on these two pages trace the growth of major airlines during the years before World War II in the United States (opposite) and other countries (below). Each bar begins with an airline's date of first service, rather than its founding date. The companies are grouped to reflect mergers. Purple bars represent carriers that eventually became part of other companies, shown on the charts in red.

Outside the United States, airlines generally underwent a process of national consolidation, and most of the lines that existed in 1940 continued to evolve after World War II (one exception: the German-run Kondor Syndikat in South America, which was shut down in 1941). But many of these groupings are shown only in purple, since it was not until later that they were known by different corporate names. The airlines of Denmark, Sweden and Norway joined together as Scandinavian Airlines System;

SCADTA and SACO became Colombia's AVIANCA; N.K.K.K. changed to Japan Air Lines; A.L.I. became Alitalia; Trans-Canada Air Lines was renamed Air Canada.

A number of the early airlines in the United States that lasted for only a few years are shown in green. And some curious duplications show up on the United States chart. New York Airways, for instance, was at first part of Pan American but was later sold to Eastern. Western Air Express is charted twice because it split into two branches, one merging with TAT and the other evolving into Western Airlines. The Delta Air Service that eventually joined American was not the same as the latter-day Delta Air Lines, though both were founded by the same resolute individual, C. E. Woolman. An even more persistent aviation pioneer was Walter T. Varney, who gave his name in turn to three separate airline enterprises.

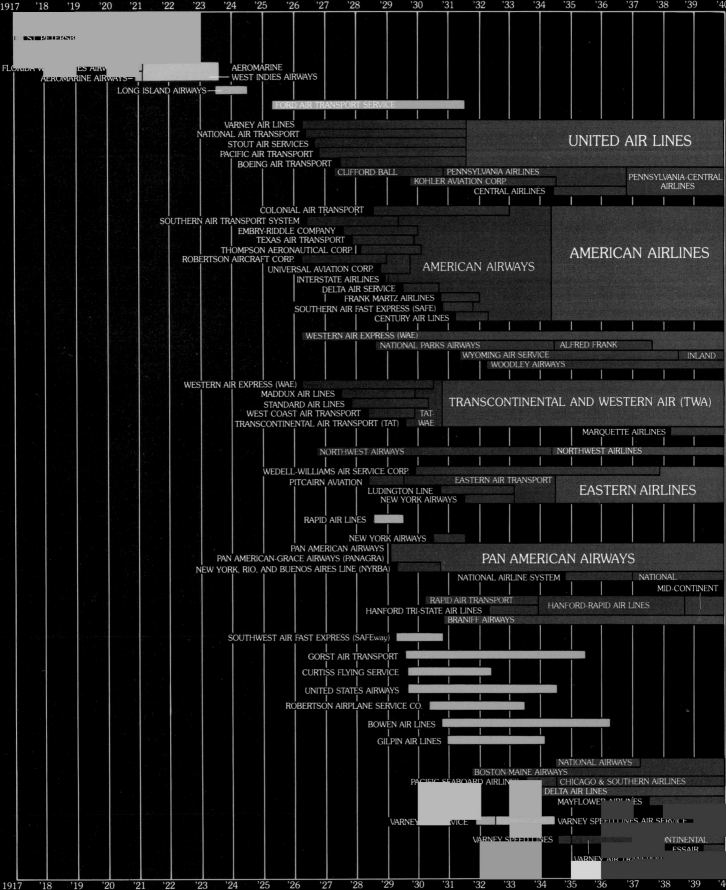

Acknowledgments

The index for this book was prepared by Gale Linck Partoyan. The editors wish to thank Frank Wootton, artist *(endpaper and cover detail, regular edition),* John Amendola, artist *(pages 108-113),* John Batchelor, artist *(pages 168-169),* Frederic F. Bigio, artist *(pages 170-171)* and Walter Roberts, cartographer *(pages 33, 101).* For their valuable help in the preparation of this volume, the editors wish to thank: **In Australia:** Sydney—J. Ball, Qantas Airways Ltd.; John Fysh; The Sir Hudson Fysh Collection, Mitchell Library; Nancy Bird Walton. **In France:** Paris— Gérard Baschet, Éditions de l'*Illustration;* Michel Hoog, Curator, Musée National d'Art Moderne; Jean Israël, Société des Amis de Saint-Exupéry; André Bénard, Odile Benoist, Elisabeth Caquot, Alain Degardin, Georges Delaleau, Gilbert Deloizy, Général Paul Dompnier, Deputy Director, Yvan Kayser, Général Pierre Lissarague, Director, Stéphane Nicolaou, Pierre Willefert, Curator, Musée de l'Air; Edmond Petit, Curator, Musée Air-France. **In Great Britain:** London— I. W. Scott-Hill, R. A. Wilson, British Airways; Arnold Nayler, Royal Aeronautical Society; R. F. Barker, Ray Lee, Anthony Harold, Reginald Mack, David Roberts, Richard Simpson, Alison Uppard, RAF Museum; John Bagley, Martin Andrewartha, Science Museum. **In Italy:** Milan—Andrea Artoni, Macchi; Alberto Menozzi,

Siai Marchetti; Maurizio Pagliano, Rizzoli; Rome—Contessa Maria Fede Caproni, Museo Aeronautico di Taliedo; Daniela Fuggetta, Alitalia; Colonel Roberto Gasperini, Stato Maggiore Aeronautica. **In the Netherlands:** Amsterdam— Fokker Picture Department; KLM Picture Department; Olga Vermuë, KLM Public Relations; Hoofdoorp—Thijs Postma. **In Switzerland:** Lucerne—Jacob Mösli, Musée suisse des Transports. **In the United States:** California— Viggo Butler, Burbank-Glendale-Pasadena Airport; Robert Ferguson, Lockheed Aircraft Corporation; Harry S. Gann, Douglas Aircraft Company; Captain and Mrs. Hack Gulbrandsen; David D. Hatfield, Northrop University; Glenn Bozarth, Linda Dozier, Western Airlines; Washington, D.C.—Christine B. Dove; Constance McHale; Susan Brown, Louis S. Casey, Philip Edwards, Robert van der Linden, Mary Pavlovich, Mimi Scharf, Catherine D. Scott, Karl P. Suthard, National Air and Space Museum; Laura E. O'Connell, United Airlines; Nick Olcott; Florida—Jim Ashlock, Paula Musto, Eastern Airlines; Illinois—Edward D. Williams, United Airlines; Maryland—Robert J. Serling; Betsy M. Snyder, Martin Marietta Corporation; Michigan— Wanda Karavas, Henry Ford Museum; Minnesota—James M. Bordon, Vincent Doyle, The Vince Doyle Collection; New York—

Geoffrey Arend, *Air Cargo News;* Katie Hill Strickler, United Airlines; Angus McClure, Rose Scotti, Trans World Airlines; Mrs. Juan Trippe; Ann Whyte, Pan American World Airways, Inc.; Oklahoma—Paul F. Kent, American Airlines; Texas—Jane Foster, American Airlines; G. Edward Rice, History of Aviation Collection, The University of Texas at Dallas; Washington—Carol Barnard, *Seattle Post Intelligencer;* Peter M. Bowers, Marilyn A. Phipps, Gordon Williams, The Boeing Company; **In West Germany:** Koblenz—Meinrad Nilges, Bundesarchiv; Cologne—Werner Bittner, Deutsche Lufthansa; Munich—Botho von Römer; West Berlin—Axel Schulz, Ullstein Bilderdienst.
Particularly useful sources of information and quotations used in this volume were: *An American Saga: Juan Trippe and His Pan Am Empire* by Robert Daley, Random House, 1980; *Airlines of the United States since 1914* by R. E. G. Davies, Putnam, 1972; *A History of the World's Airlines,* by R. E. G. Davies, Oxford University Press, 1964; *The Plane That Changed the World: A Biography of the DC-3* by Douglas J. Ingells, Aero Publishers, 1966; *The Seven Skies: A Study of B.O.A.C. and Its Forerunners since 1919* by John Pudney, Putnam, 1959; and *Airways: The History of Commercial Aviation in the United States* by Henry Ladd Smith, Alfred A. Knopf, 1942.

Bibliography

Books
Aircraft Year Book, 1928-1941. Aeronautical Chamber of Commerce of America.
Armstrong, William, *Pioneer Pilot:* London: Blandford Press, 1952.
Borden, Norman E., Jr., *Air Mail Emergency 1934.* Bond Wheelwright Company, 1968.
Bowers, Peter M., *Boeing Aircraft since 1916.* Aero, 1966.
Brooks, Peter W., *The Modern Airliner: Its Origins and Development.* London: Putnam, 1961.
Burden, William A. M., *The Struggle for Airways in Latin America.* Council on Foreign Relations, 1943.
Cate, Curtis, *Antoine de Saint-Exupéry.* G. P. Putnam's Sons, 1970.
Cobham, Alan J.:
    A Time to Fly. London: Shepheard-Walwyn, 1978.
    Australia and Back. London: A. & C. Black, 1926.
    My Flight to the Cape and Back. London: A. & C. Black, 1926.
Corporate and Legal History of United Air Lines and Its Predecessors and Subsidiaries, 1925-1945. Twentieth Century Press, 1953.
Courtney, Frank T., *The Eighth Sea.* Doubleday, 1972.
Cunningham, Frank, *Sky Master: The Story of Donald Douglas.* Dorrance and Company, 1943.
Daley, Robert, *An American Saga: Juan Trippe and His Pan Am Empire.* Random House, 1980.

Davies, R. E. G.:
    Airlines of the United States since 1914. London: Putnam, 1972.
    A History of the World's Airlines. Oxford University Press, 1964.
Davis, Kenneth S., *The Hero: Charles A. Lindbergh and the American Dream.* Doubleday, 1959.
De Leeuw, Hendrick, *Conquest of the Air: The History and Future of Aviation.* Vantage Press, 1960.
Farley, James A., *Behind the Ballots: The Personal History of a Politician.* Da Capo Press, 1973.
Finch, Robert, *The World's Airways.* London: University of London Press, 1938.
Fleury, Jean-Gérard, *La Ligne de Mermoz, Guillaumet, Saint-Exupéry et de leurs Compagnons.* Paris: Gallimard, 1939.
Foulois, Benjamin D., and C. V. Glines, *From the Wright Brothers to the Astronauts: The Memoirs of Major General Benjamin D. Foulois.* McGraw-Hill, 1968.
Francillon, René J., *McDonnell Douglas Aircraft since 1920.* London: Putnam, 1979.
Frank, John P., *Mr. Justice Black: The Man and His Opinions.* Alfred A. Knopf, 1949.
Freudenthal, Elsbeth E., *The Aviation Business from Kitty Hawk to Wall Street.* Vanguard Press, 1940.
Froesch, Charles, "Before and After the Jets Came." Unpublished manuscript, no date.
Fysh, Hudson, *Qantas Rising: The Autobiography of the Flying Fysh.* Sydney: Angus & Robertson, 1965.

Gibbs-Smith, Charles H., *The Aeroplane: An Historical Survey of Its Origins and Development.* London: Her Majesty's Stationery Office, 1960.
Glines, Carroll V., *The Saga of the Air Mail.* D. Van Nostrand, 1968.
Glines, Carroll V. and Wendell F. Moseley, *The Legendary DC-3.* Van Nostrand Reinhold, 1979.
Grooch, William S.:
    From Crate to Clipper: With Captain Musick, Pioneer Pilot. Longmans, Green, 1939.
    Winged Highway. Longmans, Green, 1938.
Hallion, Richard P., *Legacy of Flight: The Guggenheim Contribution to American Aviation.* University of Washington Press, 1977.
Harper, Harry, *The Romance of a Modern Airway.* London: Sampson Low, Marston & Co., 1930.
Hegener, Henri, *Fokker—The Man and the Aircraft.* Aero, 1973.
Higham, Robin, *Britain's Imperial Air Routes 1918 to 1939: The Story of Britain's Overseas Airlines.* Shoe String Press, 1960.
Hill, Roderic, *The Baghdad Air Mail.* Longmans, Green, 1929.
Holland, Maurice, *Architects of Aviation.* Duell, Sloan and Pearce, 1951.
Hudson, Kenneth, *Air Travel: A Social History.* Rowman and Littlefield, 1972.
Hudson, Kenneth, and Julian Pettifer, *Diamonds in the Sky: A Social History of Air Travel.* London: Bodley Head, 1979.

Ingells, Douglas J.:
  L-1011 TriStar and The Lockheed Story. Aero, 1973.
  The McDonnell Douglas Story. Aero, 1979.
  The Plane That Changed the World. Aero, 1966.
  Tin Goose: The Fabulous Ford Trimotor. Aero, 1968.
Instone, Alfred, *Early Birds: Air Transport Memories 1919-1924.* London: Western Mail & Echo, 1938.
Jablonski, Edward, *Seawings: The Romance of the Flying Boats.* Doubleday, 1972.
Jackson, Ronald W., *China Clipper.* Everest House, 1980.
Johnson, Robert E., *Airway One: A Narrative of United Airlines and Its Leaders.* Lakeside Press, 1974.
Josephson, Matthew, *Empire of the Air: Juan Trippe and the Struggle for World Airways.* Harcourt, Brace, 1944.
Keats, John, *Howard Hughes.* Random House, 1966.
Kelly, Charles J., Jr., *The Sky's the Limit: The History of the Airlines.* Coward-McCann, 1965.
Knott, Richard C., *The American Flying Boat: An Illustrated History.* Naval Institute Press, 1979.
Lewis, W. David, and Wesley P. Newton, *Delta: The History of an Airline.* University of Georgia Press, 1979.
Leyson, Burr W., *Wings around the World.* E. P. Dutton & Company, 1948.
Lindbergh, Charles A.:
  Autobiography of Values. Harcourt Brace Jovanovich, 1978.
  The Spirit of St. Louis. Ballantine Books, 1974.
Macmillan, Norman, *Sir Sefton Brancker.* London: William Heinemann, 1935.
Mansfield, Harold, *Vision: The Story of Boeing.* Duell, Sloan and Pearce, 1966.
Mason, Francis K., and Martin Windrow, *Know Aviation: Seventy Years of Man's Endeavour.* Doubleday, 1973.
Migeo, Marcel, *Saint-Exupéry.* London: Macdonald & Co., 1951.
Miller, Ronald, and David Sawers, *The Technical Development of Modern Aviation.* Praeger Publishers, 1970.
Morris, Lloyd, and Kendall Smith, *Ceiling Unlimited: The Story of American Aviation from Kitty Hawk to Supersonics.* Macmillan, 1953.
Moore, Byron, *The First Five Million Miles.* Harper & Brothers, 1955.
Morgan, Len, *Famous Aircraft: The Douglas DC-3.* Arco Publishing, 1964.
Mosley, Leonard, *Lindbergh.* Dell, 1976.
Munson, Kenneth:
  Airliners between the Wars 1919-1939. Macmillan, 1972.
  Flying Boats and Seaplanes since 1910. Macmillan, 1971.
  Pictorial History of B.O.A.C. And Imperial Airways. London: Ian Allan, 1970.
Nayler, J. L., and E. Ower, *Aviation: Its Technical Development.* London: Peter Owen/Vision Press, 1965.
Newton, Wesley, P., *The Perilous Sky: U.S. Aviation Diplomacy and Latin America 1919-1931.* University of Miami Press, 1978.
Oh, How We Flew 1926-1976. Western Airlines.

Olley, Gordon P., *A Million Miles in the Air: Personal Experiences, Impressions, and Stories of Travel by Air.* London: Hodder & Stoughton, 1934.
O'Neill, Ralph A., *A Dream of Eagles.* Houghton Mifflin, 1973.
Palmer, Henry R., Jr., *This Was Air Travel.* Superior Publishing, 1960.
Pearcy, Arthur, *DC-3.* Ballantine Books, 1975.
Penrose, Harald, *British Aviation: The Pioneer Years 1903-1914.* Aero, 1967.
Pletschacher, Peter, *Grossflugschiff Dornier Do X.* Stuttgart: Motorbuch Verlag, 1979.
Pudney, John, *The Seven Skies: A Study of B.O.A.C. and Its Forerunners since 1919.* London: Putnam, 1959.
Rae, John R., *Climb to Greatness: The American Aircraft Industry, 1920-1960.* The M.I.T. Press, 1968.
Raymond, Arthur E., *Who? Me?* Unpublished autobiography, no date.
Reilly, H. V. Pat, *A Pictorial History of Teterboro Airport 1918 to 1976.* Teterboro Aviation Hall of Fame.
Rickenbacker, Edward V., *Rickenbacker.* Prentice-Hall, 1967.
Roseberry, C. R., *The Challenging Skies: The Colorful Story of Aviation's Most Exciting Years 1919-1939.* Doubleday, 1966.
Ross, Walter S., *The Last Hero: Charles A. Lindbergh.* Harper & Row, 1968.
Rowe, Basil L., *Under My Wings.* Bobbs-Merrill, 1956.
Rumbold, Richard, and Margaret Stewart, *The Winged Life: A Portrait of Antoine de Saint-Exupéry, Poet and Airman.* London: G. Weidenfeld and Nicolson, 1953.
Serling, Robert J.:
  From the Captain to the Colonel: An Informal History of Eastern Airlines. Dial Press, 1980.
  The Only Way to Fly: The Story of Western Airlines, America's Senior Air Carrier. Doubleday, 1976.
Shamburger, Page, *Tracks Across the Sky: The Story of the Pioneers of the U.S. Air Mail.* J. B. Lippincott, 1964.
Smith, Henry Ladd, *Airways: The History of Commercial Aviation in the United States.* Alfred A. Knopf, 1942.
Solberg, Carl, *Conquest of the Skies: A History of Commercial Aviation in America.* Little, Brown, 1979.
Stroud, John, *Annals of British and Commonwealth Air Transport 1919-1960.* London: Putnam, 1962.
Sykes, Frederic, *From Many Angles: An Autobiography.* London: George G. Harrap & Company, 1943.
Taylor, Frank J., *High Horizons: Daredevil Flying Postmen to Modern Magic Carpet—The United Air Lines Story.* McGraw-Hill, 1962.
Templewood, S. H. V., *Empire of the Air: The Advent of the Air Age 1922-1929.* London: Collins, 1957.
Thomas, Lowell, *European Skyways: The Story of a Tour of Europe by Airplane.* Houghton Mifflin, 1927.
Trans World Airlines Flight Operations Department, *Legacy of Leadership.* Walworth Publishing Company, 1971.

Turner, P. St. John, *Pictorial History of Pan American World Airways.* London: Ian Allan, 1973.
U.S. Senate, Seventy-Third Congress, *Hearings Before a Special Committee on Investigation of Air Mail and Ocean Mail Contracts. Part 1. September 26 to October 6, 1933.* U.S. Government Printing Office, 1933.
Vecsey, George, and George C. Dade, *Getting off the Ground.* E. P. Dutton, 1979.
Wachtel, Joachim, *The History of Lufthansa.* Cologne: Lufthansa German Airlines, 1975.
Warner, Edward P.:
  The Early History of Air Transportation. Norwich University, 1938.
  Technical Development and its Effect on Air Transportation. Norwich University, 1938.
Weiss, David A., *The Saga of the Tin Goose: The Plane That Revolutionized American Civil Aviation.* Crown Publishers, 1971.

Periodicals
"Airways of the United States," *Aviation,* November 1934.
"Colossus of the Caribbean," *Fortune,* April 1931.
Davies, Ron:
  "The Airlines: The Early Days," *Aviation Quarterly,* Vol. 2, No. 3, Third Quarter, 1976.
  "Pan Am's Planes," *Air Pictorial,* September-November 1967.
Edgerton, Joseph S., "Seeing America from the T.A.T.," *The Aeronautic Review,* August 1929.
  "40 Years on: The Story of KLM, Royal Dutch Airlines," KLM Royal Dutch Airlines.
Gann, Ernest K.:
  "The Line," *Flying,* June 1974.
  "The Tin Goose," *Flying,* August 1974.
Gardner, Lester D., "German Air Transport," *Aviation,* July 18, August 1, 15, 29, 1927.
Grey, C. G.:
  "Uncivil Aviation," *The Aeroplane,* April 9, 1924.
  "On the World's Longest Airway," *The Aeroplane,* February 18, 25, March 4, 11, 1931.
Larkins, William T., "The Aircraft History of Western Air Lines," *American Aviation Historical Society Journal,* Spring 1976.
LeShane, Albert A., "Colonial Air Transport Inc.," *American Aviation Historical Society Journal,* Winter 1973, Spring 1974.
Miller, William Burke, "Flying the Pacific," *The National Geographic Magazine,* December 1936.
Moss, Peter W., "Wings for the Empire," *Aeroplane Monthly,* January-May 1974.
"No. 1 Airplane Company," *Fortune,* April 1932.
Schoonmaker, Frank, "Icarus Incorporated: The Reich Takes to the Air," *Outlook and Independent,* July 24, 1929.
"Success in Santa Monica," *Fortune,* May 1935.
Taylor, H. A.: "Boeing's Trend-Setting 247," *Air Enthusiast,* February-May 1979 and "Ford's Stout-Hearted Trimotor," *Air Enthusiast,* October 1978-January 1979.
Time: April 6, May 11, May 18, 1931; February 26, 1934; November 30, 1936; April 5, 1937; July 3, 1939; July 28, 1941; February 16, 1959; May 17, 1968; October 1, 1973.

Picture credits

Index